HEATHER BRAY

KEYS TO WISDOM

BUTTERFLY PRESS

Butterfly Press
PO Box 257
Blue Waters
Marazion
TR18 9AD

www.keystowisdom.co.uk

British Library Cataloguing-in-Publication Data
A catalogue record for this book is available from the British Library

Disclaimer
The contents of this book do not constitute medical advice, nor are they intended
to take the place of a doctor and the services of a qualified healer, who should be
sought for medical conditions. Also note that crystals are powerful, do not abuse
them.

Cover design by Heather Bray.
Front cover painting, "Ancient Temple by Heather Bray.

Photographs by Barrie Bray.

First published in Great Britain in 2005 by
BUTTERFLY PRESS

THE MORAL RIGHT OF THE AUTHOR HAS BEEN ASSERTED

ISBN0 9550954 0 9

Printed and bound in Great Britain by R Booth Ltd, Penryn Cornwall

"I would not" says Socrates, " be confident in everything I say about the argument, but one thing I would fight for to the end, both in word or deed if I were able – that if we believed we should try to find out what is not known, we should be better and braver and less idle than if we believed that what we do not know it is impossible to find out and that we need not even try."

- The Meno.

DEDICATION

This book is dedicated to my husband Barrie, our two lovely daughters Lucie and Vania, all the many special people whom I have met through Healing over the years, and last but not least, all the many Helpers, Guides and Angels it has been my privilege to work with from the World of Spirit.

In 1989, two years after her death, I asked my daughter, Vania, for a maxim for Life. A maxim is a piece of wisdom, expressed in a sentence. This is what my pendulum spelt out. "By adjustment do we learn our lessons".

CONTENTS

My altar, where I place the names of people who ask for help through me.

INTRODUCTION

When we pick up a book for the first time we are curious. Something has drawn us towards it. You will be wondering what this book can offer you. Is it a good read? Can it impart new and useful information to you? Is it worth adding to your collection? I believe it can be all of these things, but you will be the judge of that, so may I introduce myself?

I am a Healer, first and foremost, who is also often called upon as "One who knows", working both in my local community and much farther afield, as distance is no problem to the World of the Spirit. You may think that here in the sophisticated Western World there is no call for such a service, but you would be very wrong. I am not working among uneducated tribal people with a simple lifestyle in some very remote part of the world, although Cornwall, where I live and work, may well feel remote to you! My clients are people who find their way to me through personal recommendation. Many come from well educated and sophisticated backgrounds. However, if they or one of their family are unwell, or if they need to know the answer to important questions in their lives, then it's often me they'll call.

I have not always had these abilities, although I was certainly extremely sensitive as a child and, fortunately for me I received very loving, patient parenting. However, it was only in my middle years, after the tragic death of one of our daughters, that my gift really started to unfold. So often dramatic occurrences in our lives, such as this, open what is known to mystics as the 'third eye', which is the invisible seer's eye in the forehead, above and between the eyebrows. It is then that we start to become aware of, and to 'see,' things which others do not.

So why have I now decided to write a book? Not from a shortage of work I assure you. In fact it took me quite a while to find someone gifted, dedicated and able enough to take over my day to day work in order to give me the necessary space to make writing possible. I have never advertised and I have always had an ex-directory number, but the telephone is constantly ringing. My purpose, however, is to help more people help both themselves and others, and on a bigger scale than has been possible up to now. I have had eighteen years and many thousands of hours work experience, helping a great many people with a wide variety of their personal problems. When people have themselves been helped, they often feel moved, in their turn, to reach out and help still more people. What I know I am both willing and able to teach. I do not want the precious methods and information I have been given to be lost, to disappear when I die. I know you can find keys to ways forward for yourself, personally, within this book. I hope it will have a permanent place on your shelf, that it will be a book that will be read and referred to many times, and even get passed to the next generation.

The particular areas this book will cover are General Divination using a pendulum, Hands On Healing, Working with Crystals for Healing and How to work with Flower Essences, in particular the Bach Flowers. Fundamental to the work is a pendulum language of intuition (to be taught from within) which is extremely comprehensive. It truly gives me the 'Keys To Wisdom.'

Here is a quote from the Bible. Corinthians Chapter 12, verses 7-11.

This quote helps me to explain what I feel.

"Now to each one the manifestation of the Spirit is given for the common good. To one there is given through the spirit the message of wisdom, to another the message of knowledge by means of the same Spirit, to another faith by the same Spirit, to another the gift of healing, by that one Spirit, to another miraculous powers, to another prophecy, to another distinguishing between spirits, to another speaking in different kinds of tongues, and to still another the interpretation of tongues. All these are the work of one and the same spirit, and he gives them to each one just as he determines."

Finally, I am not a 'Faith Healer'. Those who come to me do not need to believe in anything and neither do you. You merely need an open mind, which hopefully leads to an open heart. I am the one who needs, and has built up through the course of my Healing ministry, an unshakeable faith in the power of the Divine Creative Mind. This I need in order to do the work at the level which I achieve these days, while at the same time realising that I am but a very small link in a long chain of Love.

Chapter One

How it all began

I was born into a Cornish family, who have lived in this county on the very 'toe' of England for at least five generations. Because my father was a Schoolmaster, I was brought up, during the Forties and Fifties, in small Cornish villages, where everyone knew each other. He was a gentle, kindly and clever man, sensitively nurturing the lives of the young people in his care, including my younger sister and I. Our mother was an attractive personality, lively and gregarious, possessing natural wisdom and, as a result, much loved by all those who knew her.

My early education was at the village schools, where my father was Headmaster. Then, at the age of eleven, my life took a new path, when I started to attend a local Grammar School, remaining there, until, at the age of eighteen, I followed my father's footsteps into a career of teaching. I trained in London, and, in 1961, returned once more to my beloved Cornwall, having obtained a post in a village primary school, teaching children of six and seven years of age. Whether I taught them more, or they me, is hard to say. I learned much and I hope they did too.

Soon after returning to Cornwall I met the young man I was destined to marry. We are together still. After seven years teaching I left school, having become pregnant with our first child, a little girl, followed five years later by her sister. This happy family situation continued to evolve until, in 1987, our beautiful elder daughter died as the result of a car accident. This was my 'wake up' call, my impetus to *really* look at things spiritual. There were two burning questions. - 'Where was she?' and 'Was she all right?' I did a lot of research into accounts of Near Death Experiences in order to find some answers, and found, what was to me, a whole new world of psychic awareness.

I read several books, notably by medical professionals, such as Doctor Raymond Moody's " Life after Life", first published in 1975, his "Reflections on Life after Life " and Doctor Elizabeth Kubler- Ross's " On Children and Death" and " On Death and Dying". These people were prepared to speak out and put their professional reputations on the line in disclosing their experiences with patients who had been very close to death. Remember, this was way back in

1987 and medical science was getting to a stage where more and more people could be brought back to life from the very edge of death. Because Moody and Kubler-Ross were well qualified doctors who were brave enough to to put their reputations on the line and speak out for the first time, their books sold in large numbers, and the whole, previously taboo, subject of death was spoken about more and more. People now felt safer to talk about their own personal experiences, no longer feeling that those around them might think them strange, or mad, and so more and more accounts emerged. I would like, at this point, to quote to you the end of an open letter, written by Doctor Kubler-Ross, to those who are suffering, or have suffered loss of a child. I think it is *so* helpful to all who grieve. It was certainly something I clung to at the time as a drowning man clings to a life raft.

" To end this letter, I want you to know that our research in death and life after death has revealed beyond a shadow of a doubt that those who make the transition are more alive, more surrounded with *unconditional love* and beauty than you can ever conceive. They are not really dead. They have just preceded us in the evolutionary journey we are all on; they are with their former playmates (as they call them), or guardian angels; they are with family members who preceded them in death and are unable to miss you as you miss them since they are unable to feel any negative feelings. The only thing that stays with them is the knowledge of love and care that they have received and of the lessons they have learned during their physical life. "

People were also kind enough to share their own personal accounts of Near Death Experiences. Here is just one, that I have permission to share with you. This person is well known to me and has been a close friend since 1983. The account was written out on the day following the experience, and a notable euphoria remained with him for about a fortnight afterwards.

30th January 1978

" I was in bed with a very high temperature and my wife had left home to collect antibiotics from the doctor a couple of miles away. Feeling none too comfortable, my eyes traversed the bedroom and I noticed that each object appeared remarkably bright and clearly defined, in spite of the poor light of a sunless afternoon.

Quite suddenly the bedroom walls disappeared and I seemed to pass through an indescribable kind of barrier. I found myself floating over a grey, lifeless and silent country. The sight of the dead remains of stunted growth filled me with great sadness. (This he feels illustrates the devastation that man is capable of causing to our beautiful world.) Then unexpectedly the scene changed, as I entered a beautiful living forest of majestic trees and colourful growth. As I moved through this delightful place, I was suddenly aware of a huge and magnificent archway ahead of me. The supporting pillars were a shining powerful mass of interwoven strands: black, yellow and purple. The jet black opening between the pillars had no gate or door and appeared to be the entrance through a great and many-coloured wall.

Looking towards the dark opening I saw a small bright light, which grew rapidly in intensity, lighting up what now appeared to be a tunnel through the very thick wall. Then quite suddenly, from the entrance, appeared the source of the light, which was in the form of a glorious celestial being. The heavenly one was arrayed in whiteness which glowed like silver, so brightly that the shape could not be easily observed, but the face (I only remember the eyes clearly) could only be described as lovely. With great joy I recognised this shining one as my guide, who came to me in an out-of-this-world experience some twenty years ago.

I felt very happy. "Come with me, I have something to show you", she said in a voice of gentle invitation.

My guide and I passed quickly through the tunnel into a blaze of glorious orange light which seemed to come from the great overhead dome. This high vast structure of golden arches was embellished with numerous blazing coloured lights, shining like jewels. There were numerous wonderful plant and treelike growths, reminding me of earth, but each was suffused with its own light. Distance in this place did not impair the visual clarity of anything. The sublime, all-embracing light was manifested love. Love was intense. I felt tremendous love, and saw love.

So this was Heaven. I knew this place had always been here, with <u>no</u> beginning and no ending. Everything was known about me; everything was known about all things.

As I was taken further I saw a group of men in white who were speaking loudly, praising the Holy One. I knew they were the prophets in the Old Testament, and I said to my Guide, " Then what the prophets said was true." " Yes," she replied . Looking around expectantly I asked, "Where is Jesus?" For a few moments my question remained unanswered. Then two figures appeared in the distance, clothed in hooded garments, one brown and one green. They appeared to be in deep conversation, and I received the impression that one of them was Jesus.

I soon discovered that my thoughts were instantly known, as while I was considering that a mistake had been made in taking such an unworthy person as myself into Heaven, immediately a very loud and powerful voice spoke. **"Man is very important to me."**

I was then shown something which appeared to be the surface of a very large sphere covered with a series of most beautifully coloured patterns. Each individual area of coloured pattern was held in position by an incredibly shining object, and as I drew nearer I realised that this object of such beauty was Man. The shape of symbolic Man was elliptical, and was in three parts: the two end portions were lovely, but the centre was truly *magnificent*. Man was revealed as the King Pin in the plan of the Divine Creator. **Spiritual man was really beautiful.**

Then, thinking about creation, again my thoughts were interrupted by that majestic, powerful voice saying, **" Here the earth was created."** This I knew was before time. ("passing time" as we know it). The voice continued, **" But in earth time the world (planet Earth) evolved over 4,000,000,000 years, and is still evolving."** I was then shown a large sphere, and saw an approximately 60 degrees section or wedge drawn out from the earth-like ball, showing creation from the centre core through rock, etcetera to life formation, the latter represented by a green band. The outer and final band was of a darker green and much larger than the "life" band, and indicated **Mankind's free will,** giving us a great number of choices.

For the third and last time the Great Voice spoke with much power, saying **"The Kingdom of Heaven is within you"**, filling me with a wonderful feeling of intense love. During the three periods when the powerful Voice spoke, I was strangely aware of the word "Logos", but was unaware of its significance at that moment. (Author's note: Logos means literally, "The word", and I believe it may link to the first verse of Saint John's Gospel , King James Version.   In the beginning was the Word, and the Word was with God , and the Word was God. In other words this *may* be the original enunciation of sound energy that started the whole creative process off.)

Three huge rays of light shone down from the direction of the great overhead dome on to a pure white surface. The rays were coloured yellow, pale blue and silver, but did not show any colour on the white surface. I knew they represented Past, Present and Future, being the " Everlasting Now" and all one to God.

I was then shown a record of my life on a kind of rectangular graph. **"This is where you are now,"** said my Guide, indicating a crack in the graph, which stretched from top to bottom near the end of the life chart.

To my request to be allowed to stay in this place of great love, I was gently told that it was not possible, as I still had something to do on earth. "You must learn", she said, " to love your fellow man".   "You will now return to earth," she added. As she spoke I saw our planet, blue and lovely, slowly revolving in space.

I was then escorted through the tunnel by my Guide in her shining beauty. Her last words were, " Do not worry: I will return for you soon."

Back in bed, I studied the room items, which were bright and clear. Just then my wife returned. As she walked into the bedroom I asked her for my medicine. She did not reply but stopped turned and smiled, and I watched her change to a girl of about 20 years. She was blonde and beautiful and covered by this orange-flame dancing light. I told her I loved her, and, looking out of the window I saw my neighbour, a retired farmer of about 75 years, who was hoeing his garden. At about 100 yards I could see the weave in his cap, and jacket of brown and greenish tweed. I knew I loved him. Immediately I found myself in his house, talking to his daughter, and I felt a great love for her too. Both father and daughter changed to an age of about 20 years, and both were covered by this same glowing orange light and appeared in youthful beauty.

My wife eventually returned, complete with medicine, and was, once more, her normal earthly self."

This wonderful old gentleman died recently aged 93 years. He had attended our local Quaker meeting for many years.

I myself had been brought up with Methodism taking a prominent place in family life, but four years before our daughter's accident we had started to attend Quaker Meeting. While still at College, I had been impressed by my Education Lecturer, who was a Quaker. I was intrigued that there is no priesthood, that responsibility for Ministry lies with the people themselves and no trained person is deemed necessary to stand between those present and the Divine Source.

There is a Friends' Fellowship of Healing, which is an international Quaker organisation, with which I am associated, but this book is about my own personal practice.

During the years since I have been working in healing, I have been privileged to help many others on their spiritual path. Love and compassion is what it's all about – that and a genuine willingness to help people. Compassion means literally, "To feel someone's pain with them," and those who become healers are those who can identify with others in this way, often through personal experience. There is no doubt in my mind at all that my daughter's death was the trigger for setting me off on the Healing path, but what was needed was both compassion and protocol. That is to say I needed a method of healing which felt familiar and comfortable to me, and with that I have indeed been provided over the years, the protocol growing as I grew.

Let me now explain the term, Ministry of Healing. The *actual* Healer is your client. They are going to heal themselves with Love, the Divine Source vested in us all, and the right kind of help and support from you The person referred to hereafter as the Healer is, in fact the Minister of Healing, that is to say, the one who administers the healing. Healing is about two people coming together as equals, with intention, plus the great mystery of Love.

There are a great many ways of going about this work. I shall explain my tried and tested methods to you, which will, I hope, give you the confidence to start, but I also want to help you to use that confidence and understanding as a springboard for your own particular ways of working, in order for you to discover your own unique potential.

Central to my work is the information received through a comprehensive language of movement. This is received via a pendulum, which *could* be as simple as a short piece of natural plant fibre, to which is attached a small stone. It isn't of course, but it could be. I use either a crystal with a special loop at the top, which is attached to a chain, or, what is known as a plumb bob, which is a regularly shaped piece of metal with a hole at the top through which can be fixed a piece of string. These are found in the wallpaper section of most DIY Stores, and are intended to check the vertical position of the wallpaper on the wall.

The language I use is, as far as I have been able to ascertain unique but, in my experience, eminently teachable. It is very logical and can, with practice, impart accurate and complex information swiftly. The information on the language is split into four sections. The Lines, or Axes you will find in Chapter Four, the wheel and its implications in Chapter Five, the circles and ellipses in Chapter Ten and the means of recording your information in Chapter Eleven.

Here is the story of my very first Healing. One day, while in Quaker Meeting, a message from Spirit dropped into my mind. This, in itself is not strange to me because the call to Ministry means that sometimes, while sitting in the gathered silence of the meeting, an insistent urge that will not be stilled comes over one of those gathered there to stand. The individual then will voice the thoughts that we believe have been given to us by Power of the Holy Spirit, to the other people there. The term "Quaker" comes from the emotional response, or quake that we feel at such a time.

This message, however, was unusual in that it was not for sharing. I was being told to go and visit a wonderful old Friend (the Quaker term we have for each other), who was ill, *and offer him Healing!* I was amazed. How could this be? I knew nothing *about* healing, or so I felt. However, I knew this man would be very kind and understanding. Also, he would be able to accept the unusual way in which my visit was initiated, being himself a Quaker. As for me, I was being nudged forward into making a commitment to Healing, and I knew in my heart there would be no turning back.

My friend greeted me warmly, and didn't have any problems in accepting either my story of what had happened in Meeting, or my very shaky attempts at healing. I, for my part, did what I have done many times since. I handed the situation over to the Divine Energy, saying in my heart, "Please show me what to do next!"

First I picked up my pendulum, using a "pinch" grip, between the thumb and first and second fingers of my right hand. I like to work with a short string or chain, so my fingers are only about five centimetres up from the "bob" itself. I feel that this gives me a more precise swing, but I doubt that I did it like that on that occasion. In fact I was so nervous, it's a wonder it swung at all!

I then held the pendulum over each bottle of Bach Flower Remedy in turn and noted its reaction. It either swung to the left for "No", or to the right for "Yes", for that was the full extent of the language available to me at that stage. (See Chapter Four). Amazing to me then, was the fact that the pendulum picked out four different remedies, each one indicative of a different state of mind, which my friend even more amazingly, understood in relation to himself .

I had with me a small empty bottle from the Remedy Set, and using a tiny funnel, which I'd brought with me for the purpose, I poured a little liquid from each of the chosen bottles into it, 1/4 of the bottle filled by each remedy. This strength I later realised, is emergency strength, and is not the way remedies are usually made up, but I told my friend to take a fresh glass of water each morning and put two drops of the mixture into it, which was fine. He was to sip from this glass during the day, at least four times. This is not how I dispense remedies now, but it was a practical solution at the time, and it worked. (See Chapter Six for more information).

Next, knowing that his problem was back pain. I asked him to show me where it hurt, and I put my right hand, palm facing, about four or five centimetres from the place he had indicated. I felt led to do that, rather than touch on this occasion, and in fact I worked at a distance of a few centimetres for several years before I eventually felt permitted to touch the physical body. Always be sensitive about touching someone anyway, both from a psychic point of view and also from the position of avoiding embarrassment or arousal, and *do* remember always to ask permission first.

Still holding the pendulum in my left hand, I watched what it did. It went from the Balance Line through a 45 degree angle to the right, and fixed on a line that I realised was to do with the Healing Energy being channelled. Why had the pendulum gone forward to this new line?

I knew the first cross, the vertical line crossed by the horizontal line, represented the two commandments given to the world by Jesus Christ....." Love the Lord Thy God" and "Love Thy Neighbour as Thyself." What cross could this new line be part of? The answer later became obvious. It was the diagonal cross, which is a frequently used symbol known to us as the kiss, the "shorthand" sign for Love, often written on greetings cards and letters, but it is composed of two lines, the one in opposition to the other. If one line represents Love, and, as I had been shown, Healing, what did the other one represent? It took me a while to decipher, but it was in fact Fear and Pain, elements of which were causing my friend's bad back. (See Chapter Four) Very interestingly, I was recently looking at the Greek alphabet and noticed that X is Chi. Chi energy systems are what I work with within the client's body.

The other interesting insight came when I was studying elementary Greek and found that the so-called diagonal cross, written X, represents C in English, and therefore represents the first letter of the Greek word for Christ, ΧΡΙΣΤΟΣ Christos, when written in Greek lettering! It was as if I was being shown two levels of consciousness, the Divine level and the level of the Divine vested in human form, Man. The balance line stands for the Divine, but the same line turned through 45 degrees gives you the Love, Gift, Truth, Healing line, man's connection with the Divine through form. Conversely, if so turned, the Material World Line reaches the position of Fear/Pain. Make of this what you will, but it is an interesting point to ponder as to where the language of the pendulum comes from.

For the moment, the same steady swing continued for several minutes from the pendulum held in my right hand, during which time my friend experienced considerable heat from my left hand, which was placed over the area of his spine where the pain was. Heat is a common emanation of healing energy. Finally the pendulum returned to the vertical Balance line, and finally to a state of rest, showing me that the delivery of Healing Energy was over. And so I had been nudged forward into making a commitment to Healing, albeit a rudimentary one, and I knew there was no turning back. I had been brought back from a place of no longer wishing to live, a place of despair, for a reason. I was beginning to understand what that reason was.

I knew also that I should acknowledge where I believed the Healing Energy had come from, but I admit I felt too embarrassed to speak it out loud, so I said, quietly, in my head, " In the name of God the Father, God the Son and God the Holy Spirit, Amen." I still use the same affirmation today, except that I now also acknowledge the Divine Feminine, and the Communion of saints, (Those devoted to the worship and service of the Divine Light in all races and belief systems.)

My affirmation now goes as follows:
"In the name of God the Father, God the Mother, God the Son, God the daughter, God the Holy Spirit, in and through the Communion of Saints, Amen
I have to say that now even this does not feel fully comprehensive enough, but for the moment it stands."

You may be wondering why I find it necessary to go to such lengths to affirm my beliefs. It is for the protection of both myself and my client. Healing necessarily opens up both my aura (protective body shield) and that of my client. It is important that they are safely sealed against possible negative energies afterwards.

To end this chapter I'd like to quote from the contemporary Irish poet/mystic, John O'Donohue, in his book "Divine Beauty" –

"When you have felt deep emotional pain and hurt, you are able to imagine what the pain of the other is like; their suffering touches you. This is the most decisive and vital threshold in human experience and behaviour. The greatest evil and destruction arises when people are unable to feel compassion. The beauty of compassion continues to shelter and save our world. If that beauty were quenched, there would be nothing between us and the end-darkness which would pour torrents over us."

Dramatic but true.

Chapter Two
How I learned to Heal

My introduction to the Doctor Edward Bach Flower Remedies goes right back to Autumn 1986, when I needed to go into hospital for an operation. A friend came to see me the night before I left home, bringing a bottle of Rescue Remedy. I had never heard of it then. She implored me to start taking it straight away and to make sure that it was given to me immediately I became conscious after the operation and was continued for several days. I made an excellent recovery and have given the same advice to numerous people since.

Only a few months later, in March 1987 tragedy struck. Our lovely elder daughter died, as the result of a car accident. She was just eighteen years old. Rescue Remedy again proved itself to be invaluable through those first unbelievable early days and nights. I also began looking at the other remedies in the set, and we started taking Red Chestnut, one aspect of which can be about unreasonable fear of something dreadful happening go those we love. We were thoroughly traumatised of course, and had difficulty, for a time, in letting each other out of our sight. This remedy also proved very helpful, and so I decided to buy a complete set of thirty eight remedies, each one designed to work on a different state of mind. I felt, at this point, that we had been put in touch with a very valuable natural resource indeed, and one which was always available, for helping us cope with the stresses and strains of life.

My introduction to the pendulum dates from even further back. In 1974 our younger daughter was born, and at the very end of pregnancy I was taken into hospital for observation. I was there for a couple of weeks before my baby was born. I was in a ward with three other young expectant mothers. One Sunday afternoon the young woman in the bed opposite me had a large family group visiting her, while that particular day I had nobody.

This must have been the point at which Fate stepped in because the elderly gentleman from this young woman's family came across and started to chat to me. This was before the days of body scans and he asked me what sex of child we thought were all going to have. I replied that we had no idea! His amazing reply was that if he only had a piece of cotton and a darning needle, which is a rather large sewing needle, he would be able to tell us!

With this sentence, from this elderly Countryman, my whole world opened up. They do say that when the student is ready the teacher arrives! He then went on to describe how he used his darning needle, threaded with cotton, suspended over hens' eggs to determine the sex of the developing chick within. He further told me that the needle would swing in a circle for a cockerel and in a straight line for a hen. After visiting time was over, I ventured this fascinating information to the others. The young woman in the corner bed said that she had heard of people who were able to foretell the sex of an unborn baby, but she believed that they used a pendulum, made from a human hair tied to a wedding ring. It was fortunate that this young woman had the most beautiful long, fair hair, and I didn't mind taking off my wedding ring in a good cause, and so my very first pendulum was created.

Then the fun began, because I had a new toy and time to play. I used the movements of a straight line and a circle that I had been given, and started on the people in my ward. The others were interested in dowsing for a little while, but I was captivated. People in other wards got to hear what was going on, became curious and came visiting me. Then the evidence started trickling through as the babies were born and my forecasts were proved correct time after time. What on earth was going on?

Nevertheless I did very little with this new found gift for years. We were bringing up our young family, and were kept very busy. However, I did buy a small plum bob, (normally used when hanging wallpaper), to use as a pendulum, and I used it to tell me such things as whether the milk was fresh or the dinner was sufficiently cooked, and, occasionally, whether one of my friends could expect a boy or a girl. Now the language of the pendulum extended a little, to include the swings for "Yes" and "No". (See the Yes/No cross, Chapter Four)

I still use plum bobs even now, although I also have crystal pendulums as well. A crystal is, I think, rather more sensitive, but also more "jumpy", and, if you are just starting out, I would advise a small plum bob (Approximately 4 centimetres long and just over 1 centimetre in cross-section, with a hole near the top through which to thread string.) obtainable at any good " Do It Yourself" shop. It is cheap, indestructible and symmetrical, so it gives you a good even swing. It also has a point on it, like a pencil, so that you can easily see what it's doing. Crystal pendulums can come later, when you are more confident with your dowsing and have learnt more of the very individual qualities of the different stones.

Now what of "Hands On" Healing. How did I first discover that phenomenon? When our second daughter was about nine and a half years old, she had a medical examination at school, and parents were invited to attend. At a certain point in the examination, the doctor asked my daughter to bend down and touch her toes. The doctor studied my daughter's back, looking carefully at the spine, and then she said, " I don't think there's anything seriously wrong (!), but I'd like you to get an x-ray on your daughter's back". A few days later we had the x-ray examined by an orthopaedic surgeon, who told us that our young daughter had a forty four degree curvature of the spine! You are, no doubt, thinking, "If that was the case, why on earth didn't the parents notice it?" The answer is that the curvature is inside the body, not outside. The cushions between the vertebrae of the spine start to thicken on one side only, and so the spine produces a vortex, or spiral. The only external evidence of this was that the spinal vertebrae seemed, on careful observation, to disappear in my daughter's case, somewhere between her shoulder blades.

I was devastated. I couldn't believe it! But of course, like all things that happen to us in life, we have to keep going, we have to cope. I was so desperate I thought of everything, including Healing, but strangely enough I didn't think of searching anyone else out to help. Instead I went into the Living Room one day and found my daughter lying on the carpet, on her tummy, engrossed in television. Perfect! I crept up behind her and, not really knowing what to do, or how to do it, I placed my hands side by side, palms downwards, about fifteen centimetres off the surface of the body, from where I knew the curvature to be. The effect was both amazing and immediate! She said, "What are you doing to my back? It's so hot!" I was being shown the very real Healing power of Love, but it wouldn't have happened if I hadn't responded to my intuition. Of course, there was a lot more work to do, and my daughter needed to wear a body support, called a Boston Brace for the next eight years, but, at the end of that time, the orthopaedic surgeon *did* say that this was the best correction he had ever known.

It is interesting to note that I was led along my path of discovery slowly but surely, the jigsaw being put together piece by piece over the years. I was picking up on the experiences my life was offering me. This is the way I still continue to work. It is very important that we train ourselves to be observant. That's the way Gift grows. In a way, however, I've done it so you don't have to, but maybe you will start with what's here in this book and take it forward for yourself. That is my heartfelt wish.

My work with crystals did not happen from the beginning of my healing ministry, although shortly after the death of our daughter I felt absolutely compelled to buy a rose quartz sphere while out shopping one day. I had no idea why I was buying it, but once again I was being led along the right path because rose quartz has a very soft and gentle feminine energy for working with problems of the heart, and my heart, without a doubt, was broken.

Later that evening when I was sitting holding the crystal, I felt what I can only describe as a 'fizzing' feeling in my hand, just as if the little bubbles in sparkling water were breaking against it. It felt good, and what's more I felt comforted. Since that time long ago I have given rose quartz pieces to many people in distress, knowing they will be helped by its gentle loving energy. It's lovely when you know a little about such things as crystals and flower essences because when friends, family members and neighbours are going through difficult times you can give such appropriate and helpful little gifts,which quite often get people interested in such things for themselves.

My considerable collection started several years later when my husband started it off by giving me a very large quartz 'single terminal' for Christmas one year. It was then that I realised that crystals could be laid on or around the body to aid the flow of positive energy. It was amazing what a difference they made to the healing. Whereas before I used them I had to wait while the negative energy in the body of my client gradually shifted around from a negative position to the positive Healing line, now it would happen, when using the appropriate crystal much faster, sometimes in one single pendulum swing!   (You will find information on the use of crystals in Chapter Nine)

And now I hear you ask, "Do I have a gift for this? Could I do what you do?" My answer would be this - Given the willingness to make the effort, anyone could learn to do a little. Having made a start, and had some success, many would be interested to take things further, especially if they could refer to this book and, maybe, there was someone around to help and encourage them. A few would go a long way, maybe even further than their teacher, because they were thoroughly in tune with their subject. In the end your method may not be the same as mine, but what I hope this book will do above all is to get you interested in the subject of Healing and if it does that for only a few then all the hard work involved in writing will have been worthwhile.

Chapter Three
Talking about Gift

What do we mean when we say that someone is gifted? We *may* mean that they are particularly good at something, but that could be a definition of talent. Gift is about more than this. A dictionary definition is 'A quality bestowed by nature.' - Chambers 20th Century Dictionary. Therefore a gift is given by some natural energy or power.' Nature', in the same dictionary, is defined as, 'The power that creates and regulates the world.' while the word 'Nature', is seen to come from 'Natus', Latin - 'To be born'. In order for something new to be born, or made manifest in the world, two energies of opposing polarities must come together in an energy fusion, thus forming a third and separate form of energy, born of the unity of the two.

This puts into words what I know to be true about Gift, that it is given in love from a Divine source, to the individual, but that individual must play their part in its development and use. It is a fusion between the Earth Being and the Divine Being (the two polarities). The fusion can happen unconsciously, by means of the One Consciousness (Un / Une - French for One), but, for it to happen at all, the Earth Being, be it human or animal, must be able to open to the Divine Source in order to receive. It reminds me of the wonderful painting by Michaelangelo, on the ceiling of the Sistine Chapel. Its title is 'The creation of Adam', and central to the painting are the figures of God, depicted flying through the Heavens towards Adam, who is lying prostrate on the ground. Their arms, hands and fingers are outstretched, so as to be almost, but not quite touching. To my mind the creative spark, in this case the Gift of Life itself, flashes between the two.

Are people born with their gift? Sometimes it would certainly seem so. If we think, for example, of child prodigies, those who are so far advanced in their field that they are ready to study mathematics at University level by the age of ten, or those who can perform extremely difficult classical music at the age of only six, it seems that they must be capable of very special intuition (meaning to be taught from within) in their chosen field. They simply know things, maybe because they have the innate ability to tune in to a certain specific part of the unconscious, that is to say, of the One Consciousness where everything is known.

Plato, the ancient Greek philosopher says in his Theory of Reminiscence 'Knowledge easily acquired is that which the enduring self had in an earlier life, so that it flows back easily.' I *also* believe that gifted beings may possibly be remembering things from a past life. I use the term 'beings' because it is possible for other creatures than humans, for example animals, to be gifted. I speak from experience, as I have been working with past life regression as a healing tool for eight years now. Notice the word, 'remember'. It is the opposite of 'dismember', the one meaning 'to take apart', and the other, 'to put together'. This is the purpose of regression work. It has the ability to fill in the gaps in the 'story line' of the individual, whether the gaps be in this lifetime or from the past (or even very occasionally, and I have had this happen, amazingly, from the so-called future.) It heals the personality by filling in different significant parts of their personal story line which have been 'forgotten', that is to say these parts cannot be recalled while in the normal state of consciousness and yet there is a feeling that *something is missing*. Remembering equates with Insight, and the other end of that particular dowsing line is Fear/Pain. Therefore you will understand that Wisdom, Insight and Understanding drive out Fear and Pain. (See Chapter Four)

People can be gifted in many aspects of life. They could, for example, have the great gift of making us feel loved and appreciated. Some people have "Green Fingers ". They *simply* know how to grow things. There are gifted people in all walks of life. It relies neither on intellectual ability nor status in society. The essential element is Love. There are gifted cooks, carpenters, doctors, road sweepers, musicians, to mention only a few. Gifted people imbue what they do with love; the Love energy actually becomes an integral part of what they practise or create and it is to this Love energy that we are instinctively able to respond. We are created by the Divine Energy coming together with the energy of the Earth, and as such we have within us what the fourteenth century German mystic Meister Erkhart spoke of as the Divine Sparklet, a little seed of Divine Energy of which we are caretakers, which could flourish or wither according to how it is cared for.

Other really important aspects of Gift are the *effort* and *determination* we, and sometimes those who care for us also, are able to expend. There is, I'm sure, a huge loss in human potential through the lack of these two very important resources. I believe everyone is born with a special propensity or inclination of mind (and Cosmic Mind), which could develop into a gift, but we need to open up and be determined, prepared to make an effort in order to fulfil the opportunity. Steadfastness and good old **'stickability'** are important ! Don't give up ! Gifts can and do develop, so give yourself time. It's never to late to start trying. Life is a journey of discovery and self discovery. There is always more we can learn. Don't let's be too easily satisfied, but strive to go further. And *please* never feel that you are too old!

So you see, your gift is there like a seed in your heart, and will it grow? Well it won't grow if it isn't tended regularly. Do you feed it with your effort, enthusiasm and love, or are you easily discouraged? When learning to dowse find at least a few minutes each day to practise. People say to me, "Oh, I can't do it!", and I reply, "Well, do you practice a little each day ?" Lack of perseverance is the biggest reason for failure that I know, not just in dowsing, but in life itself. **Somehow people expect to be able to dowse expertly immediately.** I have found that my particular gift of Healing grows through observation, examples of which you saw in the previous chapter. Taking note of what is happening and of what my guides are telling me is important, and so the range of the gift is expanding all the time.

I have introduced the word, "Guides." What do I mean by that? You will remember that I spoke of gifts as being of a Divine nature. Anyone who is gifted, in whatever field, will have had the experience of doing something that is of a better quality than they, by themselves are capable. This suggests to me that the work is guided. I choose to personify the energy of that help, because it makes it easier for me to relate to. Also, it makes changes in the 'feel' of a particular energy easier to both relate to and explain. Simply, a different guide is in place.

How do I know that my work is guided? Of that there can be no doubt. When someone comes to me, or talks to me on the telephone, and I can tell them many things about themselves which are of an intimate nature, without them telling me anything at all except their name, no other conclusion is possible. This happens consistently, time after time. The person, or animal, for I work with animals as well, could in fact be anywhere in the world. So how are they identified? Information is held in what I think of as the Divine Mind, so I only need a simple piece of information to key me into that person, such as their name, and/or the area, or even country where they live, and, of course, their permission, to download information which is relevant to their well-being. How do I obtain an animal's permission? Animals, I have found, are extremely open and receptive to healing, and all that is required of us is an openness of mind and heart.

The key is, most usually, the person's first name. Of course this could be a very common name, such as Mary or Peter. How does the Divine know to which Mary or Peter I am referring? Well, we are all, individually, **known, loved and understood.** There are no exceptions to this. Obviously some of the things we do are not loved, but our connection to the Divine is non- negotiable. We are known by the Divine Mind better than we are known by our nearest and dearest friend or relative, better even than we know ourselves. I have had proof of this many times, but conversely our whole lives are voyages of self discovery. There are two important questions, **'Who am I?', 'What am I doing here?'**

If I didn't know the person's name, then something as seemingly vague as the gentleman from Liverpool, or even the little girl in France, would be sufficient. How do I know that this is so? I know because the information can be substantiated. That is the individual's assurance, and mine, that what I say is happening is really happening. I am telling you this, not just because you could be working in this way some day, but also to show you the extent and detail of the Divine overview.

How do I arrive at the information and why am I permitted to receive it? The information is received through the many and varied swings of the pendulum. It is the simplest of tools, and so its use would always have been possible, right back to Stone Age times. I am able to receive the information because I strive to be impeccable in my practice. Impeccable comes from the word impeccant, without sin. Sin is a 'loaded' word for lots of us, but it actually is a term from archery and means to miss the mark. So it means to make an error, or mistake. I am not saying I am impeccable, simply that **I try to be** and I will endeavour to show you how to be impeccable also. That is, I will show you how to dowse without making mistakes. We will start to discuss the various movements of the pendulum in the next chapter.

How did I acquire such a language? It was through watching and listening, picking up clues here and there and gradually putting the jigsaw puzzle together. This was a good thing, because the developing language paced my emerging gift. It probably took about three years for the full language to emerge, and, even then, a few more insights came later, one even after I started writing this book! The point I am making is - Be observant, question things.

Now let's talk about how information is stored. The truth is that everything is known about everything! No wonder the image of a single eye has often been prevalent in popular mythology and even in places of worship. There has long been a feeling among spiritual people of all persuasions that we are being watched over. Of course the implications for all of us, in this, are enormous. And now you've read it here you can no longer say you didn't know!

There is a huge library of information, known as the Akashic Records, so you see, the folk tale of us all having a Book of Life is, in essence, true. Akasha is a Sanskrit word meaning the place where thoughts and feelings gather. Sanskrit is one of the oldest languages in the world. The reason that this very extensive record is kept is not, I believe, judgemental, but is in order that our mistakes may be shown to us later on, in the space between lives, in order to help us go forward constructively and not destructively. Interestingly, it has been reported that we are shown there what it is like to experience our actions, or non-actions, from the other person's point of view. Also our true intention behind our actions is known and is very important. What was our motive? Did we do what we did through Love or was there a negative intent?

Life is a school, where, hopefully, we learn our lessons. It is a fact that in general terms every person who has ever come to me has come with the same problem. That is they are somehow somewhat 'stuck' in their lives and are finding it difficult to go forward, so you may feel comforted to know that there is such care and concern taken over each and every one of us. Because the record is so comprehensive and thorough I, and people like me are able to access very precise information on someone, in order to help them go forward. This is similar to how I believe it is in the space between lives. Records may be referred to and errors pointed out. The light is on. Everything may be seen. Each one of us is known, loved and understood, but true love is about discipline and correction too.

Here is a quote from the Bible, New International Version. This is from The Book of Proverbs Chapter Nine, verse eight.

"Rebuke a wise man and he will love you.

Instruct a wise man and he will be wiser still.

Teach a wise man and he will add to his learning."

It is certainly true that the difficult times in life, such as serious illness and bereavement, can be times of huge learning, instruction and correction in our lives, as can those times when someone speaks their truth (how they see the truth from their viewpoint) to us, in a kind but firm way.

It is important that people ask for help in connection with healing, but the asking may, at times be tacit. That is to say it may be silent or unspoken, but unless they "let me in" at some level of their consciousness there is no way that confidential and personal information can be reached. The level of information reached varies according to the healer's level of experience. We undergo certain initiations or experiences as we walk life's path, and, while I believe we're all, in truth actually walking the same path (and I agree that some of us are certainly dawdling, if not walking backwards!), we can certainly be seen to be at different stages along it, so for anyone to try to find out information about another person, without truly loving and wanting the very best for that person is foolhardy. Our motives are seen, as well as our actions known, so while you might get an answer, if your motives were not good it wouldn't be the correct one. And if at any point your pendulum refuses to move, you will know that you have either overreached your ability, gone into a 'No Go' area, or have asked a question that doesn't need answering at all, because you already know the answer!

As well as working with Guides, who are Light Beings at a very high level, good dowsers need to work with a Guardian on their channel. (See Chapter Seven) This is to guard what information is being given, and to whom. This is an absolutely essential filter on the system. Of course, information, once received, needs to be recorded accurately and stored safely. (See Chapter Eleven.)

Finally, a warning. I am always **very respectful** of the world of Spirit, just as I try to be to those in incarnation. There is the complete spectrum of Spirit Energies all around, from the shining bright to the very dark, so always work for the **best and highest good and not for any particular outcome,** then you won't go wrong. Remember there is a karmic law that what you give out, although it might take time, you get back!

Chapter Four

An introduction to the pendulum language - The four crosses

"If we do not expect the unexpected, we will never find it." - Heraclitus

A few years after our daughter's death a dear friend of mine who lives in Dorset gave me a birthday present of a visit to a Medium. This lady was able to tell me many accurate things about my life and family and then she said, "I have a young woman here who says she is your daughter. Do you have a daughter in Spirit?" She described our daughter and went on to say, "She's holding up an equal armed cross enclosed within a circle and she's telling me that she works with this energy." Amazed, I answered " Well *I* work with that energy!" You will see that the medium was accurately describing what I call The First Cross and her words to me helped confirm what I already believed to be true, that my daughter is working with me.

Our home is very close to Saint Michael's Mount, where there are several ancient granite crosses, but one in particular is known as the Mount Cross, and sometimes as, and I quote - The "mystic cross, upon which weeds and lichens never grew" (Whitfield 1852, 7). The upper, most prominent cross on this ancient standing monument **is an equal armed cross within a circle**.

There were unusual circumstances around us coming to live in this very special place. In January 1988 we were attending a Christmas party at the house next door. We had no knowledge or connection whatever with the house where we now live, and it is not, in fact, visible from there. My husband just happened to overhear our host mentioning to someone that the lady next door might be selling her house some time in the near future. We, at the time were looking to find a way forward for ourselves and our younger daughter and were drawn more and more towards the Penzance area for the art, spiritual connections and schooling. This caused my husband to mention to our host, "If the lady next door would like to sell, we might be interested." It was nine months later when we received a telephone call from the owner saying, " I believe you would like to buy my house." Up to this point we had not looked at the house, not even from the outside! We came down one very rainy day to take a look and all fell in love with the place. It then took us a further whole year to purchase and renovate the house, but considering everything that has happened since, we feel that we are definitely meant to be here! I *do* feel very linked with the Archangel Michael energy and sense tremendous support from the fact that this sacred place has long been associated with Healing, the Oracle, and the equal armed cross within a circle.

Please Note: There is generally no significance in the sizes of diagrams throughout this chapter.

THE FIRST CROSS

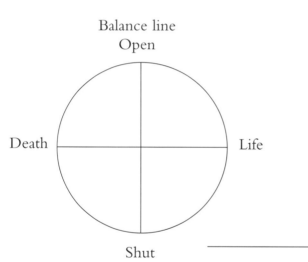

Divine Connection/Material World

Balance.

Divine Connection.

At One With Source.

Unconditional Love.

Neutral Position

Material world and

Personal Relationships.

Conditional Love.

Physical or Psychological

Death.

No way through/the closed

door.

PLEASE NOTE THAT THIS FIRST CROSS REMAINS ON EACH OF THE THREE FOLLOWING DIAGRAMS OF THE CROSSES AS GUIDELINES FOR YOUR DOWSING

I am occasionally asked if it matters whether or not I am sitting facing directly forward, as far as the pendulum is concerned. It is interesting to give a little demonstration to show that it does not. The pendulum is shown in fact to have the ability to follow the edge of a piece of rotated card, once the Balance Line is established, regardless of whichever way or at whatever speed the card is rotated. The command is simply "Balance".

The rectangle represents the piece of card being rotated and the pendulum swing will track the edge of the card as a fixed bench mark.

The pendulum is held in a 'pinch' grip, between the thumb and first and second fingers of the, in my case, right hand, although it could be that a few of you are left handed dowsers.

I like to keep the string short, to a distance of maybe only 4 or 5 centimetres, but you must always remember to use the length that feels right for you.

Card seen in horizontal plane.   Pendulum working in vertical plane

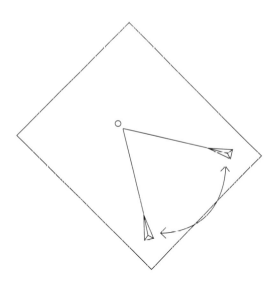

When a client comes to me for the first time, I need to show them how the pendulum responds to me. If I think "Balance" the pendulum starts to swing to and fro in a measured way, towards me and away from me. This is represented by the vertical arm of the first cross. The pendulum continues to swing in this way for as long as required, which is an unusual phenomenon, because the friction which occurs, (I pemanently have a small calouse on the outside edge of my index finger.) does not stop the pendulum from swinging.

Sometimes it swings for one piece of information or another for most of a two hour session, *however* long it is needed and in continually changing patterns of information!

When working in Healing, Balance is a very important term. It represents the Middle Way of Buddhism that which leans neither towards affirmation nor negation, because these only exist relative to each other, and therefore neither has any independent reality of its own. Notice the other meanings this line also has. It is the situation of Ease as opposed to Disease. Disease is literally Dis-ease," being uneasy, being stressed, being unhappy and so on. If these negative energies remain unresolved in our body's energy field, or aura for any length of time, they may well lay down a disease pattern in the physical body itself. This does not necessarily happen immediately, in fact it can take as long as two or three years to manifest, and so preventative procedure is a very real option. Also of course, in the favourable conditions fostered by Natural Healing methods, the body has an excellent opportunity for regeneration. (Incidentally, the pendulum continuing to swing, unaffected by friction, suggests there is ease rather than dis-ease occurring in this phenomenon also.)

Negative energy which left unchecked leads to disease, is always on the look out for a weak point in the aura (the energy field which envelopes the whole body for its protection). If the aura can be sufficiently energised, made positive, which means in pendulum terms that the energy reading would be anywhere from the Balance Line to the Healing Line, then healing could occur. The further towards the Healing Line the energy is, the *faster* healing can occur. (See following diagram.)

How is the energy raised at any given point on the body? This can happen by placing one or both hands on the body, or at a small distance above the body, with the *intention* of healing.

Alternatively it could be achieved by placing an appropriate crystal on or beside the body, in a given location, as you may instinctively be led to do. Your pendulum may help you decide which option to take. The crystal acts as a key hole or rite of passage to the Healing energies invoked and the particular characteristics of those Healing energies will be in accordance with the inherent qualities of the crystals chosen, although your use of them, like mine, may be an instinctive rather than a intellectual choice. (Refer to Chapter Ten on Crystals.)

I hold the pendulum in my right hand and, using the index finger of my left hand as a pointer, I move over the area of the body on which I am working, watching for the moment the Truth line is reached on the pendulum. This will be the specific place at which I need to be working, using one of the methods explained above.

Diagram showing the Healing Line

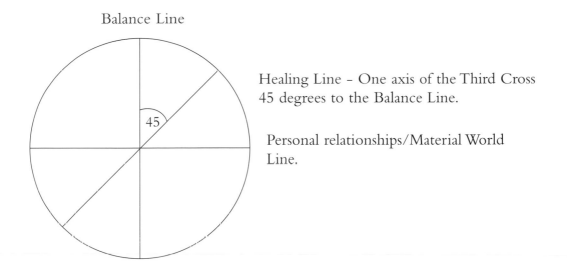

Balance Line

Healing Line – One axis of the Third Cross 45 degrees to the Balance Line.

Personal relationships/Material World Line.

The above diagram also shows the Balance Line, in its positive manifestation, represented on paper as a vertical line, and standing for the healing energies of serenity and ease. It is the link with the Divine Energy, being as we say "At one with Source". This is the perfect state and is only attainable, at best intermittently, but we strive to achieve it. Any line of course has two ends, and for dowsing purposes each line has a name. The upper end of our Balance Line we will call Open and the lower end we will call Shut. This expresses the positive and negative polarities of the Divine Energy.

Next let us consider the horizontal axis of the first cross. It balances the vertical axis and has a temporal quality against the spiritual quality of the former. This represents links with the material world, with personal relationships, and with Conditional Love. It contrasts against the spiritual relationships, otherworldly links and Unconditional Love represented by the vertical axis. It also represents the qualities of duality. One end we call life and the other death. This axis can also, in some instances, mean a closed door or an open door. In a Christian sense, this first cross also represents the two great commandments of the Prophet Jesus, "Love the Lord thy God." and "Love thy Neighbour as Thyself"

I know it is very challenging to consider the duality of the Divine, the qualities of Black and White, Life and Death, Open and Shut. However, no doubt you will have heard the terminology, Christ and Anti Christ. If you think of Light and Dark or Yin and Yang, the ancient Chinese philosophy of the two opposing but complementary forces at work in nature, it may help you to understand that without the one we are not able to perceive the other. Behind the world of duality however, there is only the one, as illustrated in the Zen Koan, the sound of one hand clapping, or the Anahata, the Sanskrit name for the Heart chakra, the seat of Love united with wisdom.

The word Anahata means the sound that is made without two things striking, or "unstruck". In other words the beginning of creation required No Thing (not the same thing at all as nothing). It was simply spontaneous. Quantum mechanics is now explaining how the Big Bang could have started all by itself. The problem is that the scientists also seem to be using this crucial piece of evidence to *deny* the existence of a Divine, all-powerful Energy. However this scientific explanation is not news to anyone who reads their Bible, where we are told in the First Chapter of the Gospel of Saint John that "In the beginning was the word (a spontaneous energy form) and the word was with God and the word was God."

Also in the Angelic Orders, as recorded by Pseudo Dionysis in the sixth century, the Seraphim, who are the First Choir in the Third Heaven, and therefore, the Angelic Host closest to the throne of God, are constantly praising God and sending out waves of Love Energy in the sound of their wings, which make the sound " Kadoosh, kadoosh, kadoosh." This sound is reminiscent of the waves on the seashore, an expression of La Mer - the sea (La Mere, The Divine Mother.) The original Dionysis is said to have been a friend of Saint Luke and there is thought to have been a long and careful tradition of passing the information down orally until it was finally written down. The keepers of the wisdom listened very intently each time the stories were told to make sure that absolutely no mistakes were made.

Scientists have also been trying to think of God only in terms of the gaps left in human knowledge, which gaps, as more and more of the universe could be given logical explanations, were thought to get smaller and smaller. The truth, in my humble experience, is that all information about everything a is held in a data base which could be said to be the mind of God, and Man is still uncovering it, but because The Knowledge is so extensive and constantly ongoing, Man can never catch up.

The universe is in a state of constant creation. God is indeed the God of the gaps, for we all have gaps in our knowledge, even the knowledge we have of our own selves, let alone others. The filling in of some of the gaps in the Soul History of an individual through Healing and Past Life Regression Therapy techniques, is in fact a most important aid to the advancement of the individual Soul. Carl Gustav Jung, the famous philosopher, believed that were people to close the gap between their ego (Who they identified themselves as being) and their unconscious minds (Who they truly were) they would return to full mental health. One of the problems until now has been how to achieve it. Who am I? What am I doing here? These are **fundamental** questions.

However it is not for me to judge others. I simply speak my truth according to my experience. When someone comes to me for healing, this is the position I hold. That person is known, loved and understood by the Divine Energy (Is held in the Mind of the One Consciousness) standing right where they are. It is my job as a healer to acknowledge that and work with it, and although we have spoken of the duality of the Divine Energy, the Absolute Truth is that there is neither Good nor Bad, Light nor Dark, Sorrow nor Joy. All things simply ARE. The judgement is in our perception, but all things serve the Divine Purpose.

The next cross is much simpler, and I'm sure, if you've tried dowsing with a pendulum before, you will have some movements for Yes and No. These movements may well be different from the Yes/No language positions that I have been using. Please do not worry about that because you realise that there is an intelligence behind the pendulum and that intelligence is capable of change. Whenever I have been teaching dowsing it has amazed my students how easily the pendulums are able to adapt from one language to the other, when required to do so.

THE SECOND CROSS – The Yes/No Cross

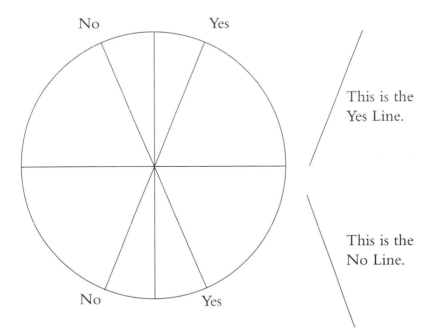

You will see that once again we are dealing with duality, simply Yes/No, and No/Yes. If both lines represent Yes and No, how do we know which is the correct interpretation? It is, in part a question of force or thrust, but in reality it is very unlikely that you are going to be dealing with the bottom half of the circle, as far as interpretation goes. The lines are named by the energies emanating in the upper hemisphere of the circle, For example the Fear/Pain Line, the Lethargy Line, the Obsession Line and so on, but the opposite ends of these lines are interesting from a point of view of understanding , insight and order as well as occasionally being important for interpretation.

THE THIRD CROSS – Fear/Pain against Love/Truth/Gift/Healing

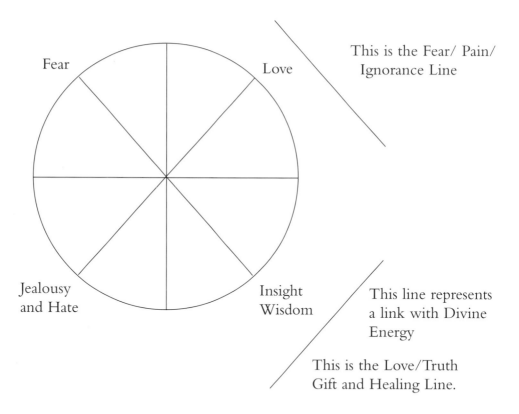

This is the Fear/Pain Line crossed with the line of *human connection, as opposed to unity* with the Divine. It represents the qualities of Love, Truth, Gift and Healing. Why are these Divine Energies interchangeable? It is because they come in on the same wavelength of energy. How do I know which interpretation to use? As in all language, it is a question of interpretation within a given context. Ask your pendulum, or your client, which word is the most appropriate. Note that at the opposite end of this line are the dark forces of Jealousy and Hate.

What balances Love is Fear and Pain, but what opposes Love is Jealousy and Hate. Fear is interchangeable with Pain in terms of energy. Once again they come in on the same wavelength. However Insight, Understanding and Wisdom are the other end of the Fear/Pain Line, opposing Fear, Ignorance and Pain. In other words, and this is a very important concept - When people understand what has been, is, or will be going on and why, they are likely to be less afraid and to suffer less pain. This is a point that many of those in authority, such as doctors, teachers and parents, for example, would benefit from taking to heart. People need explanations for things, This is, in fact, a very important part of Regression work. Often there is an ill-defined fear, concern or pain that something threatening will happen in the future, when in fact it may well be shown through regression techniques to have happened in the past.

Take as an example a person who has a severe, debilitating fear of heights. They may well be shown that they did indeed die from falling from a great height at some time in the past, maybe even in the far distant past, hundreds of years ago. The miracle is that once they are allowed briefly to relive that experience, in what they know to be a safe environment, in the company of a regression therapist whom they trust, the fear dissolves.

The counterbalancing line to Fear/Pain you will remember is the line of Love, Truth, Gift and Healing. It takes a very powerful energy indeed to counteract those. They are opposed by Jealousy and Hate. Fortunately only very rarely have I come up against a force this negative. We often use the word Hate when what we really mean is Dislike. How would you realise the interpretation of the line?

By context.

By directional thrust of the pendulum swing.

By ASKING a) Your client; b) Your guide, through the pendulum, using only the Yes and No lines! Your guides are there, at your side, to HELP you, and you do not need to feel that you must know all the answers. Involve your client, get them talking. As in life itself - If you don't know, ask!

I would like also to express my concern at the attitude of certain doctors and therapists who seem to insist in spelling out the very worst case scenarios possible, and striking deep fear into the hearts and minds of their hapless clients. These people carry tremendous authority and power, and they say that this or that WILL or WILL NOT happen - This child will not walk. That person will end up in a wheel chair. And so on........ The truth is they cannot and do not know! I have seen many miracles, and, when the person is given hope and support. insight and understanding, then ANYTHING can happen. Why don't we just wait and see?

Let us discuss the energies of Love, Truth, Gift and Healing with you a little more at this point. They bring to mind that wonderful painting on the ceiling of the Sistine Chapel, painted by the gifted genius Michaelangelo. Its title is "The Creation of Adam", and, central to the painting are the figures of God and Adam, God flying through the air, Adam lying prostrate on the ground. Both figures have fingers, hands and arms outstretched, almost but not quite touching. To my mind, the creative energy, which cannot be seen, flashes between those two outstretched fingers, but there remains a GAP. That gap, and that energy which cannot be seen, is of fundamental importance. This is the place of the Minister of Healing. Power, the power of **Unconditional Love** has a channel or conduit through which to flow. This is why we must quash any sense of self-importance about the work. The energy is simply passing through us. It is not from us, but *through us.* We need to be as pure a channel as we can be so that we are able to access and carry energies of a high vibration. In our gifted moments the self-same thing is happening. We are used as channels to bring the formless into form, so be sure to work with an open heart and and an open mind. I often get asked if Healing tires me. Actually research has shown that there are health benefits for both the Healer and the Healee. Certainly there are wonderful benefits in terms of job satisfaction. In fact, I personally think it is the best job on earth!

And what of Truth? My pendulum spends a lot of time swinging on this line, and so that the client will recognise the line, I often illustrate its position at the start of a session. The reason this line is so fundamental is not so much, as you may be thinking , to ascertain whether or not my client is telling the truth, although it does fulfil that function, but rather **whether my translation from the language of the pendulum into the spoken word is accurate.**

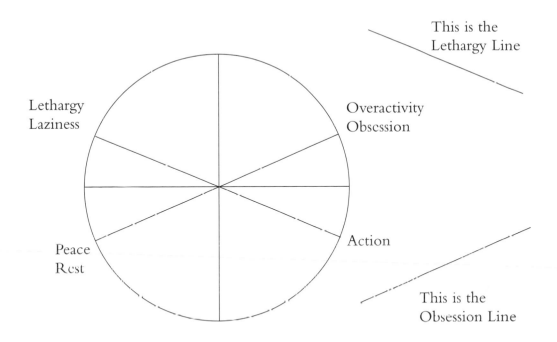

This is the crof of Lethargy and what I term Obsession. I must point out that I am not using the word in its clinical sense. Instead I am expressing a sense of "Love gone too far", the situation , in its most extreme form, of a person doing something or for example, loving someone to the exclusion of almost everything else, in fact of having almost no energy for anything else, and so you can see how these two energies of Energy and Obsession balance each other.

Obsession is then opposed by the energies of Peace and Rest, while Lethargy is opposed by Action.

You will see that Action works in opposition to Lethargy and Laziness, while Over Activity is balanced by Under Activity. Correspondingly Action is balanced by Peace and Rest, but Peace and Rest are opposed by Obsession. Opposite ends of the same line we say are in opposition, while energies on either side of the Balance Line are in balance. Very soon you will be able to see how all these energies fit together, and understand the logic of it all, although, for me, intuition came first when all this was coming into form, and logic followed. That is to say, it was only when the four crosses had been put together that the logic behind it all became obvious.

Now let's look at the Obsession Line. The other end of this Line is Rest. Very interestingly, this is the next position on from Death, or A Closed Door, on the wheel, the wheel being what the circles and Lines become when they are superimposed upon each other. (See Chapter Five) The circles become the rim of the wheel and the lines or axes become the spokes of the wheel. It is important that you remember the word AXIS as I shall be referring to it frequently in the future.

The pendulum language takes a bit of learning, but it is very much worth the effort, because it is your **key to wisdom** and being able to follow everything I do. I advise that you practice regularly and have some **fun** with your pendulum. We have been talking about very serious subjects in this book, but I also have a very light-hearted side. Remember the saying, "Angels can fly because they take themselves lightly." Ask some questions to which you already know the answers, or get someone to hide something in your room or in the garden, but only in a small area to begin with. Try to keep your mind blank. Don't try to think the answers out. Gift is specifically about NOT doing it thinking. When you think, Logical Left brain gets in the way of Right Brain intuition. Remember what that means - To be taught from within. One final point - don't get obsessed with it. Remember that obsession is Gift gone too far!

The language that I have explained in this chapter represents half of the total protocol. For the second half of the pendulum language, please refer to Chapter Ten, "Circles and Ellipses", but I want to warn you not to try to go ahead too fast. You will be wise to make sure that the information discussed in this chapter is well understood and practised before proceeding further. You can do a great deal with just the **Yes / No cross**. In fact, as I've said before, many good dowsers work solely with that. Remember the old proverb "More haste, less speed." In the next chapter I shall be discussing what I call the wheel, which shows all four crosses superimposed on each other, and in Chapter Seven you will find the Spiritual Protocol necessary for your success with dowsing, how you can find a guardian for your channel and the five important questions to ask before you begin dowsing. Also you will find help and advice for using what you have already learned so far.

Authors tip: Trace the lines of these pendulum language diagrams with the tip of your finger to accustom yourself to the movements involved.

Chapter Five
The Wheel and its implications
– Advanced concepts

"God is the God of order and not of confusion."   Isaac Newton

Imagine for a moment an old fashioned balance scales. In order for the horizontal bar to remain so, what is in one pan must equal what is in the other.

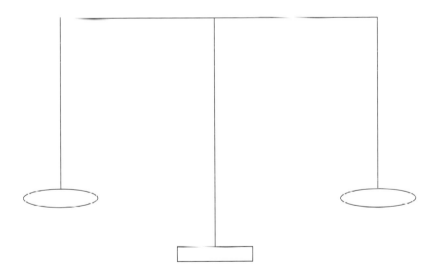

Everything on the left of the vertical balance line is counterbalanced by opposing energy on the right. When Yes and No are of equal energy (or weight) they "cancel each other out" and we have balance again. In other words, it is neither yes nor no, it simply *is*. This is something Mystics have known for a long time: things are neither good nor bad, they simply are.

We should not judge, and the more we have grown spiritually, the less we are inclined to point the finger at others, for we cannot know to what difficulties and hardships they may have been exposed. Instead we accept the situation as it is and try to move forward from it.

This is the position I take when I am working with clients. The challenge is to eventually draw a line under the wrong doings of the past and move on, either by self help or help from others. Life is full of challenges and hurdles. Can you cope? This is the underlying reason why every one of my clients has ever visited me. They are stuck in some way, unable to move forward and they realise they need help in order to be able to do so. They are, to use a metaphor, thirsty, and I need them to understand that I am the tap and not the water. The help they undoubtedly get comes through me but is not ultimately from me.

The Balance Line represents our unity with the Divine Energy, but our *experience* of the Divine is through the opposing energies on *either* side of that line. We experience the Divine through both love and pain, life and death, action and rest.

When studying the wheel it is important to note the order of the words written around the circumference of the wheel. If we take negativity - that is to say "No" for example, we can see that negativity gets to 45 degrees from the Balance Line before the Fear/Pain line is reached. Also note that the "No" position is operational all the way from just to the left of the Balance Line right down to the Fear/Pain line itself, although for convenience I place it at 22.5 degrees left, in other words there are degrees of No, (negativity) as well as degrees of Yes, (positivity).

Similarly there can be degrees of Fear/Pain/Ignorance and also degrees of Lethargy. This being so, it is possible and beneficial to **deal with negativity in the mind before it induces the onset of pain in the body.** Remember negative thoughts create a negative energy field, and a negative energy field deters healing. Negative thoughts need to be recognised, discussed and released.

As with negativity, so with positivity. There are degrees of positivity, right up to the Love Line. After the Love Line however we border on obsession, degrees of which exist all the way down to the horizontal Personal Relationships/ Material World Line. In other words, the Balance Line and the Line of Love, Truth , Gift, Healing would seem to have a special quality in that they operate on singular and specific wavelengths, the one on the Divine Level and the other on the Earthly Level.

I think the amount of time I spend on each session surprises people at first, but I am looking for a permanent healing, with understanding, and not a superficial "patch up". Wisdom and understanding are the main aims of the work, and out of this grows a sense of self-empowerment. Also there are a lot of tools in the tool bag and many avenues we can pursue. Clients soon discover that an unrushed, relaxed atmosphere is important, that the flexibility of my work plan is important, and that a session of two hours duration, because it has been enjoyable, has flown by. However in the early days of my practice when protocol was simpler, sessions of one hour duration were sufficient.

There are other correlations, such as positivity leading to Love, Love going too far and becoming Obsession, and Fear/Pain leading to Lethargy or Laziness because it stops us doing what we would secretly love to do.

Going back to the Life /Death line, there are some interesting placings here also. For example, the next position to Death is Peace and Rest. If Peace and Rest are bypassed, the individual may be holding on to very strong emotions such as Hate, Jealousy, extreme negativity, or even relentless love, and so hugely resists moving on. This explains the occasional need for exorcists, who know what powerful sacred language and rituals to use in order to help the lost soul on its way to a place of support and education. Usually extreme measures are not necessary and with suitable help and encouragement the discarnate entity is ready, for itself, to move on. We remain stuck, both in this world and the next, until we are ready to accept and work with our situation, so do at least try to forgive and forget, and put the past behind you. Each day is a fresh start. Remember there is no true forgiveness if you are not able to forget and, most importantly, that includes forgiveness of oneself. The two things *do* go together – forgiving and forgetting. If you find this impossibly difficult, look into your heart to discover why. What you find there will not be Love and remember that to cut yourself off from Love is to eventually cut yourself off from Life

You will see, on the lower right hand side of the wheel, the words **insight, action, life**. This term 'life' may be in the sense of taking an energetic interest in life once again after a fallow period, such as a retreat or even a bereavement. However, it may have otherworldly sense about it: of **insight** and **wisdom** gained through regression experiences, or experiences such as one would receive in the space between lives, leading to **action** and the will to step, once again, into incarnation and literally be born again.

Finally, let's talk about the bottom end of the Balance Line, called Shut. When we are in such a frame of mind we feel shut down, thoroughly miserable, cut off from Life and from those around us. There may well be those people around us who are willing and capable of helping us, but they do not succeed in doing so, however hard they try, until we reach out to them. No matter how bad we feel, it is we ourselves who must reach out our hand to receive help. Then, once we become more positive, represented by the next line end to the right, the Yes, we can begin to receive Insight and Wisdom, (one more move to the right,) Insight and Wisdom hopefully leads to Action and Action leads to us being able to get back into Life (the open door) once more. We will have moved through four distinct stages, represented by these four positions to the right hand side around the wheel.

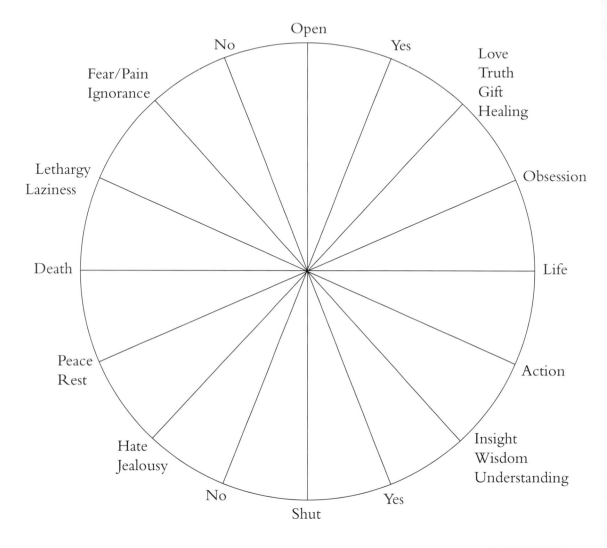

Normally I am only working with the top half of the circle, but it is important to know the meanings of the opposite ends of the lines.

This is the wheel and is a diagram that I hold in my mind while dowsing. It is composed of the four crosses superimposed on each other.

Note that the root of ignorance is "ignore" – to willfully refuse to look.

Some Healing examples

Now that we have lots of different lines or axes, how do we use them? Fundamentally we use them as a means of bringing about Balance, or at least bringing us closer to that desired state, for longer periods of time. Balance is a perfect energy state, alignment of energy through all the different chakras, or energy centres of the body and in all the different levels of mind, giving us an alignment, through Spirit, to Source, or our Higher Self if you prefer that term. It is what we aim for but only occasionally are able to achieve. Nevertheless it is the bench mark against which everything is measured. It occurs when our energy is in alignment with the Divine Energy and many people nowadays, both Eastern and Western, use methods of meditation in our busy modern world, as a means of achieving this sense of Unity, of being at one with our True Self and all things. When healing however, it is an important achievement to get your client's energy on the Healing Line.

My using so many terms for Balance is because it is a difficult concept to explain. These are only words in a book, and as such, at best, they can only come somewhere near what I know to be true. People can be so sensitive about terminology and I am trying to be sensitive around your feelings. After all, at the end of the day, if you have read this far, whatever way we would choose to describe the Infinite, we are likely to be talking about the same thing. Whatever spiritual path we follow, if we are truly working with Love then I believe we are going the same way.

As far as my own Healing work is concerned, one purpose, among several, for the pendulum language is its use in conjunction with the Bach Flower Remedies. To give you an example of the horizontal line in use, we will take the Beech remedy. This remedy in general terms, is, and I quote Doctor Bach, " For those who need to see more good and beauty in all that surrounds them." If the pendulum gave me the horizontal line over these printed words, and remember this line stands for Life/Death issues, Personal relationships/ Material world problems or an Open and Closed Door situation, possible translations *could be* -

   a) that my client was having a difficult time in their personal relationships,

   b) that they had experienced difficulties and possible malpractice in their business affairs.

   c) that someone had treated my client meanly and had "shut the door" on them.

   d) that the horizontal line stood for someone's death , and because of grief, my client had become disillusioned, and how could a loving God possibly be allow this to happen?

The pendulum allows you to get close to the problem and the more experience you have the closer it is possible to get, but it deals in general areas and not necessarily specifics. Having got the general area right, the client will usually need to fill in the specifics.

Being faced with these four options that have been intuitively given to me, the client may or may not react to one or more of them. They might, for example, say, "Yes, my daughter died last year and I'm finding it very hard."

However if they do not react, or indeed speak, we need to find the correct interpretation, the truth, via the pendulum and the No Line, the Yes Line, and if you are more experienced with your pendulum, the Truth (Love/Gift/ Healing) line as well. The answer could be one or more of the above-mentioned possibilities. The context of the session may well indicate a clear cut answer, or the answer could be indicated to me by the pendulum going straight over on to the Truth Line. Having silently established the problem I would start making gentle enquires.

However, it might be a combination of factors. for example my client may have experienced both a) and b), shown above. They might have experienced difficulties in business deals and then, because of the stress, their marriage was in difficulties. If this was indeed the case the pendulum would give me the Yes Line for both a) and b) but neither, on their own would be indicated by the Truth Line. Put the two together however and you get the **whole** truth. The pendulum goes from Balance to Yes for a) and from Yes to Truth when you add b).

Now I know this is a complex, advanced exercise, and of course if you are a beginner, I don't expect you to be able to manage it, but I want this to be a book that will last you and your family for many years, a book that allows you to grow in ability and to which you will refer time and again. Just for the moment it may be wise to simply enjoy reading and work out the complexities as you feel ready to do so. You will be learning all the time anyway.

Lets take another example of how you could do this work in a slightly less complex way. You will have to hand your copy of " THE TWELVE HEALERS, and other remedies." by Edward Bach, and for this method you will also need, "BACH FLOWER THERAPY, The Complete Approach." by Mechthild Scheffer.

First, instruct the power behind the pendulum clearly what you want it to do, for example, "Give me the Truth Line." Get that established first, so that the pendulum can consistently find you the Truth Line, not at this stage asking it any questions. For the moment its just establishing the 45 degree angle of the line. You see, it's a bit like training a puppy. You have to be clear in your instruction at first, and be prepared to repeat and practice things until you, your guide (more of this in the next chapter) and your pendulum get used to each other.

Next, using THE TWELVE HEALERS, and the Yes/No cross, pass the pendulum over each paragraph referring to a specific remedy, in turn, asking it to pick out every remedy that you need. If you get more than six, you would need to go through the **selected group** again, using the Yes/No cross to weed out those of lesser importance at the moment. Let's say that we now have

Mimulus, Cerato, Honeysuckle, and Wild Rose. You would read the descriptions of each of the remedies to your client and discuss their reaction to each in turn. Maybe there is one remedy, that from the description already given, your client cannot relate to and that the remedy is Wild Rose. The description in THE TWELVE HEALERS book is as follows:

"Those who without apparently sufficient reason become resigned to all that happens, and just glide through life, take it as it is, without any effort to improve things and find some joy. They have surrendered to the struggle of life without complaint."

You might think that is quite a challenging proposal to put to someone, and of course they could be in denial of their situation, but it's more likely, if they don't respond, that they truly do not relate to what you have said. After all they have come to you for help and hopefully respect you. Even if I thought they *were in denial,* I would still kindly challenge them by saying that this is the information I am being given and can they understand why I might be getting it? The aim is to work *with the client.* Let them know from the beginning that you are going to work on these problems *together, as equals.*

Next you turn to the MECHTHILD SCHEFFER book and turn up the section on Wild Rose. Now you have much more information to hand. You ask the pendulum, using the Yes Line (or Truth Line if you are able), to pick out the paragraph or part paragraph that your client needs to hear. You do this by passing the pendulum slowly down over the text, in a vertical direction until it starts to move from the No Line position towards the Truth Line.

It might be interesting for you to know that my guides are actually feeding me these examples and the pendulum has given me the following paragraph –

"A baby that has been crying for its mother for hours will at some point give up hope of its mother ever coming to relieve its hunger. Feeling utterly deserted and in complete emptiness it becomes resigned to its fate. Interest in life disappears. What is left is someone who merely vegetates, without energy."

Now these are only words in a book on the one hand, and on the other hand they are keys into this person's mind through memory and experience. I would read the whole paragraph out loud so that there was a "lead in", but the pendulum actually goes over on to the Truth Line at, "What is left is someone who merely vegetates, without energy." This particular sentence has now been highlighted. If this were a real life situation I could guarantee that my client would now understand the situation. They might say something like, "My parents ran a busy business and had very little time for me. I was left in the care of my older sisters who didn't really want to be bothered with me. They wanted to be off with their friends. I think my parents were too busy to notice, but I was often left alone in the house, feeling sad and lonely. I've always wondered why my energy levels are low, because the doctors can find no physical cause for it, but this helps me to understand."

Once the trapped emotional energy is converted into sound, verbalised, spoken about, the block in the Chi energy of the body clears, at least to some extent. This is an example of Insight pushing out the Fear/ Pain of childhood, of filling in a missing piece of the jigsaw of understanding, of bringing a difficult childhood memory up from the subconscious or unconscious levels of the mind into the conscious level, talking about it to someone safe and so processing and releasing the mental block. Therefore, this insight in conjunction with the person actually taking the supportive Wild Rose remedy which has been identified, improvement, sometimes dramatic improvement, in their energy levels could ensue.

Our job is to "turn up for work" and not think things out, but trust that we can be, and *will* be, guided in what to do. Make an affirmation or say a prayer for help before you begin if you like, that you may be guided in ways that will help this person in the very best way, not to any particular outcome but working always, with your guides, for your client's best and highest good. Remember "As above, so below." You do your very best and the guides will do theirs.

Of course any one of the lines in this section of the pendulum language could show itself . It is not just that a remedy is picked out, as when using only the simple Yes/No cross. Now it is also the line the pendulum swings on *while* picking a remedy out. For example, the pendulum swinging on the Obsession Line over the Willow Remedy. Any line which presents itself is noted (see chapter eleven on hieroglyphics). Your job is to detect any line or movement other than the Balance Line. We are necessarily identifying any negativity, in order to be able to convert it to positivity. or positivity in order to improve it. Transformation is what we are about.

Remember not to read the text relating to the remedy until later. We are developing Right brain, not Left brain. Do not think about it, just hold the name of the remedy in your mind, which is linked to Cosmic Mind, and watch for what your guide or guides are giving you, as if it were on a blank screen, or shown in a pool of still clear water. The following is a quote from the final page of a book written by Alexandra David-Neel and Lama Yongden, entitled, "The Secret Oral Yeachings In Tibetan Buddhist Sects." "To go beyond knowledge" means to immerse the mind once more in it's original virgin world which, like space, can contain all because it is void. The "going beyond", the "non-activity" are the means for us to attain mental freedom. In truth we have nothing to *do,* it is more a question of *"undoing",* of clearing the ground of our mind, of making it, as much as possible, clean, void. The void is, here, for us always a synonym of liberation".

Learning to clearly see and to really hear is what this job is about. Pay attention to those words dropped into your head and cross check for the truth by means of the pendulum. Know that you can also ask for a guide who is an expert in your client's problem to be in attendance for example paediatrics or orthopaedics.

The Willow Remedy we were discussing stands for:

"Those who have suffered adversity or misfortune and find these difficult to accept, without complaint or resentment, as they judge life much by the success which it brings. They feel that they have not deserved so great a trial, that it was unjust, and they become embittered. They often take less interest and are less active in those things of life which they had previously enjoyed."

If the pendulum swung on the Obsession Line over this one you could have a compounded situation, because the Obsession Line is always balanced by the Lethargy Line. OBSESSION IN ONE AREA OF A PERSON'S LIFE BRINGS ABOUT LETHARGY IN OTHERS. Anyone who is obsessional or over energised in one area of their life will have their energy depleted, be lazy, in others. Obsession, in this context, is love gone too far. I am **not** talking about repetitive obsessive disorder here.

This person is known to be less interested and less active than they should be anyway. I think in such a situation there could be much needing to be discussed because you have a double negative, of lethargy on lethargy or inactivity. If I turn to the Mechthild Scheffer book again on this one, I am given - (and I am *actually* being guided through these examples) "Willow is a state in which disappointments and resentment are powerfully projected onto the outside world. Essentially it is commonly seen in people who have passed the midpoint in life and unconsciously realise that only a few of their ideals and hopes have been fulfilled."

It is now easier to see why the client might be almost overwhelmed with emotion over this.

As the word "unconsciously" has been highlighted, you can see once again how important it might be for your client that you at least have been told, through the pendulum, what is going on. You can then begin to talk to the client, which helps process and release the energy block. You can also give them the emotional support of taking the particular remedy, and you can encourage them that life is not over, that there is still time to do something about the situation. They *could* still learn to drive, take up painting, or organise a visit to America to visit their daughter!

I do hope these examples do not seem too difficult for you. Of course they are going to seem complicated at the moment, but they show something of what can be done in the future, and for now you can achieve a lot of very useful work if you can only manage Yes and No, so do get started!

It might be both interesting and enjoyable to share this journey of discovery with a friend, working through examples and exercises together.

Chapter Six
Beginning the Practice of Healing

That day, long ago, when I received a message in the Meeting House, to go and offer our friend Healing, never having done such a thing before, I was, I'm sure, being guided. There comes a time in the lives of all budding healers when we feel we are being moved to offer our help to someone. When this time comes, remember that it is important to act from a place of compassion and humility. Also, understand that your offer may not necessarily be accepted, although if you are sensitive enough about your offer, it almost certainly will be. I expect you are thinking, "But surely people should ask for help ?" The thing is they won't be able to ask for help from you until they know of your interest in Healing.

You know how we may be moved to put an arm around someone who is upset, or how a mother may pick up a small child who has fallen, and kiss it better. Healing is an extension of that. It's just that the Healer has learned a few more things to do. The Bach Flower Rescue Remedy, for instance, would be most helpful in many cases, and all that is necessary is to have some at hand. It comes in three forms, liquid, spray and as a cream. I know people who never go anywhere without some in their pocket or bag!

The next thing would be to familiarise yourself with the qualities of the other remedies in the set, numbering thirty eight in all. The little book I have always used in my practice is called, "The Twelve Healers and Other Remedies" by Edward Bach. It is a very slim volume, bright yellow in colour. I like to use it because it offers classically simple explanations of all the Remedies, written by the great man himself. This little book was published back in 1933, when only twelve of the thirty eight remedies had been discovered, but, at this point in time Dr Bach felt that he had found something too important to keep to himself any more and went public. I have used this little volume so much I have worn out two. You may wonder why I recommend several books to you throughout this little book. It is because healing is about information and education. I don't need to hold all the information in my head, but I *do* need to know how and where to obtain it!

Just to give you a little background on Edward Bach, he was a well-qualified medical doctor, who just after the First World War, was working in hospital as a bacteriologist.   Bach discovered that poisoning from certain organisms in the intestinal tract was the cause of chronic disease and when these toxins were removed, the so-called chronic complaint disappeared. Hahnemann, the Father of Homeopathy, from his investigations many years before, had realised the same fact.

Bach was a very gentle man and his aim in life was to heal people of their ills by the   gentlest of means. At first the vaccines to remove the toxins were administered by injection, to be followed later by administration by mouth, as it caused the patient less stress. He always worked to promote ease and not disease. The medical profession sometimes seem to feel it necessary to spell out the "worst case scenario", often thoroughly traumatising the patient and their family, maybe without realising it and, I'm sure, setting up a whole host of potentially harmful negative vibrations. I have often had to work with the aftermath of this, usually with considerable and sometimes truly amazing improvement for the people concerned.   Please don't let's underestimate the power of encouragement and praise, or indeed expectation, in healing.

Of course, many doctors are gifted healers themselves but we should not put them, or indeed anyone else on a pedestal and I do wish that more of them would be prepared to at least look at the marvellous results alternative working methods can also achieve. It would be wonderful if we could all work together more. Dr Bach said, back in the 1920s that medical doctors were dealing with secondary emanations, not primary causes. We need to get to the psychological root of what is going on with an individual and work with that. Also, it is vital to take into account the temperament of your client. We are all individuals, and therefore medication, ideally, would be designed for each individual, Designer Medicine, as it is now rather smartly called. Working with Dr Bach methods, this dream has long been a reality.

Bach classified the enormous variety of organisms present in the intestines into certain groups by means of their fermentation action on sugar, and divided them into seven main groups, which included most of the organisms found. The seven groups of bacilli he named :
1. Proteus.
2. Dysentery.
3. Morgan.
4. Faecalis Alkaligenes.
5   Coli Mutabile.
6. Gaertner.
7. No. 7.

The property of the vaccines prepared from these groups he found to be that of purifying the intestinal tract and of cleansing and keeping pure all that was eaten, so that what left the body was wholesome and inoffensive. The seven bacterial groups correspond to the seven different and definite personality groups formulated by Bach and known as nosodes.

These are :

1. For those who have fear.
2. For those who suffer uncertainty.
3. Not sufficient interest in present circumstances.
4. Loneliness.
5. Oversensitive to influences and ideas.
6. For despondency or despair.
7. Over-care for the welfare of others.

He was soon able to predict, from the personality of his patient and their symptoms, the organism to be found. However this method of treatment by injection was too painful and so, after much research, the gentle, easily administered flower essences evolved.

More information on this fascinating subject can be found in Chapter Five of the book – The medical discoveries of Edward Bach Physician.

In my experience, my client usually needs remedies from more than just one category. Also, remember that at the next session it is usual for a different group of remedies to be selected, because the person will be in a different emotional place. The goal posts of life will no doubt have moved.

However, if you want to discover just one main remedy for someone, use your pendulum to go through the seven nosodes, picking out just one group. Follow this up by going through all the remedies in this selected group, again picking out just one. You could do this if you are only able to work with the Yes and No lines, but the resultant remedy could prove very helpful and insightful. You would probably need to explain to the pendulum at the onset that you only wanted one item identified each time.

For example, let's say the group your pendulum picked out, by giving you Yes, was Group 5, Oversensitive to influences and ideas. You would then turn to that group and hold the pendulum over the name of each remedy in turn. This time Holly has been picked out. (My pendulum is actually picking these things out at this moment.) However, let's say that when I read the short paragraph in "The Twelve Healers" book the person does not understand, and, as you know, the understanding of why they need the remedy is important, so we must turn to the other main source book that I use, Bach Flower Therapy by Mechthild Scheffer. We turn to the chapter on Holly and the important message for our friend is picked out, and I quote:

"We should develop a keen ear for people who say they are so tolerant that they know no jealousy. It is highly improbable that this is a serene, wise person. One would rather suspect that he has already gone so far towards death in his heart that he no longer is able to suffer and to love.

From this point of view it is always reason for rejoicing when Holly comes up in the diagnosis, for it shows that there is a potential in this essential point that is still capable of development, for the person is longing for love and will also be able to give love".

Well! That just shows you how amazing all this is! I set out to give you a simple example of the work, but the guides have another agenda and present an example of a remedy which could, all by itself, be literally a life and soul saver!

The little yellow Doctor Bach book that I work from is a "must have" for what I do. The "Bach flower therapy, the complete approach" by Mechthild Scheffer is also essential. As you have already seen, this is a book I often turn to if I'm trying to establish exactly what the client's problem is, or find very specific areas of help. Say, for example, we are shown the Lethargy Line on Elm, which is about feeling depressed, or disheartened because you want to do something you consider to be really useful in the world, but the task feels overwhelming. As we are shown the Lethargy Line, obviously the client's energy is low, but we still want more information. What do I do? I simply turn to the Chapter on Elm and trawl down through the script, without reading it, getting the pendulum to pick out, by means of the Truth Line, further information to which the client will invariably be able to relate. Once again this example was chosen, not by me, but by my Guides. In the Mechthild Scheffer book, these two sentences were highlighted: "The Elm Flower energy has aptly been termed 'psychological smelling salts'. Elm will lend strength to the strong in moments of weakness." You can imagine what good psychological, as well as practical help information like that can be to the person who is struggling. They realise the information is coming, not from me but through me, so they really feel that someone somewhere knows what they are going through and is going to help them, which, of course, is how it is. I find, in teaching, that it is impossible to waste energy in mere examples. When demonstrating healing, or getting other people to practise it, always some act of healing takes place.

When you start dowsing all you need to use are the Yes/No cross and maybe the Balance Line. Just for fun it would be good to try working out some Remedies for yourself. Start at the beginning of your book, with the Fear group and simply work through. Do NOT attempt to read each paragraph. This is a Right Brain intuitive exercise, not a Left Brain logical one. More thorough, exacting working practices are explained in Chapter Seven. See how well your guide and pendulum know you already. If **not** very well you feel, then you had best give them more opportunities to get to know you better!

The pendulum language is very useful for information on other things but those directly linked to healing, although they are linked to well-being. It will pick out suitability and quality, for example. If you choose to do this, start with small things to which you already know the answer. Is my car in the garage ? Do I like spinach? Should I buy this book? Is this a good quality bottle of wine and will I like it? If I were dowsing in this way, I would expect to see the Truth

Line. We also use it to decide on dates for holidays and times of trains and aeroplane flights, and it's useful to decide whether or not I will be pleased with a purchase when I get it home. Be careful how much you use the pendulum for these things because it is not good to get too dependent on it and always bear in mind that it is very moral **and literal.** When we visited Venice a few years ago we were travelling in quite a large party. When we got to the airport we were told that the plane was delayed. People were hungry and several of our party wanted to go to the local trattoria for some lunch. My husband asked me what time the plane would be leaving. The pendulum told me 2.30pm. As it was only just 12.30pm we seemed to have plenty of time and so off we all went. We had just finished eating and one of our group came rushing in, "Hurry, hurry," he shouted, "our flight has just been called." We all got on the plane and my husband said to me, "You're wrong *this* time!" The engines started up and we just got to the end of the Perry track when the announcement came. We had not been given clearance over French air space and we sat on the end of the runway until **exactly 2.30pm**, when the plane took off!

Also, as you gain in experience, you will come to understand that there are degrees of Yes, degrees of No, degrees also of Lethargy and Obsession. Each of the axes, or spokes of the wheel, are marked out at distances from each other of 22.5 degrees, but actually Yes can vary all the way from just past the Balance Line, to just before the Truth Line, that is from Plus 1 degree Right to Plus 44 degrees Right. In other words there are degrees of Yes but the truth is always the Truth. Conversely, there are degrees of No or negativity, but Fear and Pain are always at 45 degrees left of Balance. After that you have Fear/Pain **and** degrees of lethargy all the way down to just above the horizontal line of the First Cross. And, of course, Balance is Balance!

It is good practice to have a neutral position for the pendulum, rather like the neutral position for the gear stick in your car. If you insist that it return to the Balance Line swing after every foray made, at least while you are a beginner, movements will be clearer and easier to see.

As you proceed in your practice you may find that your guide is trying to extend the range of information received. The pendulum may start to swing, for example, on the Fear/Pain line or on the Obsession line. Remember once you manage one skill they will lead you on to another! You have seen that it is not just that the pendulum swings over a remedy but that it swings in a particular way, thus imparting additional information, and once they have passed you one piece of information be **observant**. They may well pass you another one directly! Always have a notebook handy to record the information you receive. When working with clients I use a Duplicate Book, roughly 12.5cms by 20cms in size, obtainable from any good Stationer, thus enabling me to give my client the top copy and retain a record for myself should I need to refer to it. I will be giving you hieroglyphs for quick, easy and accurate recording of information in

Chapter Eleven, and a design for a record keeping tabulation at the end of this chapter. You may prefer this as being clearer than my duplicate book scribbles, but whatever you use, do keep a copy.

While on the subject of recording information, I would encourage you to get a small indexed box file and a set of cards. When you start to work with a new client, always take details as follows :

Full name. Address. Telephone numbers, e-mail address, if appropriate. Also just a brief statement, in a few words, of why the client feels they need to see you. Get them to verbalise this themselves.

This card is used for jotting down information such as medication details, key names of people in the family, brief progress reports etcetera. Each time a client visits, have their card before you, so that you can appear efficient and well informed.

It is important, of course to try to get your client to talk to you as much as possible. You are working, on the issues being raised, together, remember. Also you need confirmation from your client of what the pendulum is telling you. Occasionally you may be working with someone who is, you suspect, in denial of an issue. They really do not want to address it. If this happens just accept the situation, but write it down anyway. There may be an opening later on in the session when the subject comes up again, and is easier to access. The important thing about getting your client to talk is that Healing is about working with the Chi energy of the body. Chi is the system of energy meridians that, from very ancient times, have been believed to exist in the body. Well-being is linked to our ability to express emotion, rather than suppress it. When we fail to express our emotions, blockages are set up in the flow of energy around the body. It is essential that you provide your client with a safe, secure environment in which to be heard. There is need for the utmost integrity in this matter. You may well have the privilege of being told things, often very private or painful things, that have maybe never before been discussed with anyone, and, as you never know when the dam is going to burst, keep a box of tissues handy! Also do not offer solace immediately. It is very important that people have an opportunity to feel their feelings and have them honoured, without them being immediately damped down, as may well have happened to them countless times before.

Write down each remedy that your pendulum picks out, together with the line it swings on. By the time you reach the end of the little yellow Bach flower book you may have accumulated quite a few, maybe as many as fifteen or so. Don't worry about this. What happens is that you receive an overview of the whole situation, some elements of which are much more important than others. It is like sweeping out the dark corners of someone's mind, getting out all the little bits into the light of day, so that nothing has been left behind, but all necessary points have been covered. At this point, and in the light of the discussion with your client, go through your recorded list again, asking the question Yes or No. Six remedies is an absolute maximum to dispense at any one time and they can all go into the one treatment bottle. This is because to use more would only be confusing to the etheric body, that is to say, the energy field surrounding the body, upon which the remedies will be working. Incidentally the pendulum has never picked out more than six remedies on a second read through, but in the early stages you may need to make this point clear to it. Information and Training!

As a final test of accuracy I start with the original All Over Energy pattern shown by my client at the beginning of the session. As each remedy is added the power of the word is shown in terms of energy as the pendulum moves closer and closer to the All important Love/Truth/ Healing/Gift Line.

If we are able to fulfil our aim of balancing the energy in the Energetic Field, thereby creating a situation of Ease, the physical body is provided with the best possible conditions in which to mend itself. This is reflected in the first stages by the person declaring themselves to be feeling more relaxed, less stressed. The aim is always to match, as closely as possible, the energy of the client's energetic field to the energy of the plant material used, in order that this very important situation be maintained. In other words the person's emotional problems are correctly perceived and matched and supported by remedies. The healing that then follows is an esoteric, mysterious and often amazing process.

This brings me to the Healing itself. In the early days I practised different methods than I do today, but the early methods, described here, were simple and effective. I will be discussing other more complex methods later in the book. There are a few simple rules to follow:

Never attempt to heal without the person's permission at some level, albeit tacit.

If you feel moved to touch the physical body, do ask the person's permission.

Never, in the early days, touch the top of someone's head. This is an advanced procedure. The crown is an EXTREMELY sensitive area. It is the fontanelle, or "soft spot" on a baby, and is said, also, to be the highest orifice through which the Spirit or Essence leaves the body at the point of death.

Work with specific problematic areas first, before working on balancing the whole body.

Let's say, for example, you have a client or friend with a stiff shoulder. If you pass your left hand, index finger pointing, over the area, the pendulum, held in the right hand, may well indicate to you where, within that area, you should be working. If this doesn't happen, get help from your client. Never be afraid to ask for help. You are not required to know everything, so just simply ask them where the problem is. People like to be reminded that the healer is human! You could then work in one of two ways. First you could drop the pendulum altogether, and, laying one hand on at the back of the area and the other hand on at the front try asking your guide, silently, in your mind, to send the Healing energy through the body from hand to hand. If, for example, your client was known to be suffering from Arthritis, you could even ask for an expert in that field to be your guide! You are not doing this work on your own, but are part of a team.

Another way of working would be to pinpoint the area for work, and, either hold your right hand flat against the body, or at a little distance, if that feels better for you, and watch what the pendulum is giving you. Do Not Do Any Thinking. This would only be ego getting in the way. Your function is to be a channel. You are the tap and not the water! Just BE THERE for that person. What might the pendulum be giving you? Well, as an example, it might start swinging on the Fear/ Pain Line, registering the pain in the area. Then, if you are not using a crystal, (with the use of a crystal it could be much more direct) it will jostle forward to the Love/Truth /Gift /Healing Line (You could even ask for that to happen) and continue to swing there, until the Healing Energy has finished being transmitted. Finally the pendulum returns to Balance to indicate completion.

Having worked on the specific body area, and incidentally, always be very careful how you deal with sensitive, sexual areas, so as not to cause embarrassment or arousal, we turn our attention to the whole body. For this, sit your client in a straight-backed chair, with shoes off, legs uncrossed, and feet placed firmly on the floor in front of them. Ask that they hold their hands out, palms upturned, in an attitude of Asking and being open to receiving, Healing Energy. Stand behind your client, and, either place **both hands** lightly, palms down, on their shoulders, whereby you will need to have a sense of when to finish, (You can check for Yes or No with the pendulum) or place **one hand ABOVE** your client's head and watch what the pendulum is giving you. It should move from a negative position on the left, to the Healing line, (If it doesn't do that, ask that it should,) and once again, swing there while the Healing Energy is being received, finally returning to Balance.

At this point, an affirmation of where YOU believe the Healing Energy to come from is called for. You could say, "In the name of........(The Creator, Eternal Divine, The Earth Mother, Father/Mother God, Universal Energy, or what ever force for Good YOU truly revere), Amen, (meaning Thy Will Be Done.)" This affirmation is necessary to protect both you and your client. The energy fields of both of you have been open and it is essential to close them down safely. (For more advanced healing methods, see Chapter Thirteen)

And what of your client? What might their experience have been? There could be so many things, but to give you some examples of the more common ones....... Heat is very common, Cold, A light breeze, Mild pressure, Tingling, Some light manipulation by other hands than yours. I have had people surprised, but never shocked by this, because they know my work is guided. If their eyes have remained closed, which is often a good idea, they may see a colour or colours, or they may experience nothing at all, and it is important to assure these people that experiencing nothing does not mean that nothing has happened! Also, let them know that the Healing does not happen for just those few minutes, but goes on for several days. Good advice for those who have just received Healing, is that they take things easy, at least for the rest of the day, even going to bed, if that is how they feel. Also, drink plenty of water, to help flush out the toxins released by the Healing. The client needs to behave responsibly, by taking the remedies regularly as instructed, drinking plenty of water, following a healthy lifestyle and taking adequate rest. Healing is very much about self empowerment. Remember, we heal ourselves, with loving help and support.

Although I have spoken in this book particularly about Bach Remedies, made by several different manufacturers because they are my preferred choice, these methods work with all brands of flower essences.

Making up the Remedy

The remedies are taken from the stock bottles and put into a special 30 ml capacity treatment bottle, obtainable from your supplier. The bottle is then filled up 1/4 full with either brandy or cider vinegar, and topped up with good quality fresh water. Do not use distilled water as this is 'dead' water. The traditional number of drops to take from each stock bottle is two, and the client is requested to take four drops as a dose, but, as it is not usual for me to see my clients more frequently than at four week intervals, and I do not wish them to be concerned about running short of remedy, I take four drops from each selected stock bottle, and the client is requested to take two drops as a dose. This, in effect, doubles the capacity of the bottle. The only time remedies are taken straight from the **stock** bottle, (the remedy as you buy it from the chemist) is when it would only be needed for, at most, a few days. The client reads and takes away the following information.

How To Take The Bach Flower Remedies

1 Two drops is a dose.

2 Drops are to be taken at least four times a day. This a minimum. There is no maximum. Just remember two drops is a dose.

3 Drops should be taken in at least a tablespoon of cold water or fruit juice. If you have no liquid vailable then two drops in the mouth is permissible.

4 If you put drops in your mouth, be careful not to touch your mouth with the pipette, or you could pick up bacteria, which could contaminate your remedy, turning it cloudy.

5 Take your remedy whenever you feel stressed, and also first thing in the morning before rising, and last thing at night before retiring. A good tip is to go to bed with a little glass containing four drops. Drink half and leave the other half for if you wake, or in the morning.

6 Take your drops between meals, at least thirty minutes from food, e.g. mid morning, mid afternoon, mid evening.

7 If you take your remedy and do not feel its beneficial effect, wait five minutes and take it again.

8 Be sure to keep your remedy in a reasonably cool place

HOW THE REMEDY IS MADE UP

Your remedy is made up in a specially produced Bach Flower Treatment bottle of 30ml size. Four drops of each chosen remedy (No more than six in all) are put in the bottle. Then the bottle is first filled 1/4 full with either brandy or cider vinegar, at the dicretion of the client. Finally it is topped up with good quality still spring water, and blessed. This is to ensure that the energy therein is optimum.

Chapter Seven

Good dowsing Practices
Working with Guardians and Guides

As Quakers, we find inspiration in many different texts, both ancient and modern, including the Bible, but I would like, at the beginning of this new chapter, to share with you a few Bible verses from Psalm 139. In the light of my experience, they mean a great deal to me.

O Lord, you have searched me and you know me.
You know when I sit and when I rise;
you perceive my thoughts from afar.
You discern my going out and my lying down;
you are familiar with all my ways.
Before a word is on my tongue you know it completely, O Lord.

These words mean so very much to me because I know their essential truth. Some people do not feel comfortable with a personification of the Divine Energy, and I respect that, but I actually find the implied intimacy of the connection very helpful. We each have the chance of establishing a personal connection to the Infinite! In fact, very early on in a session with a new client, the pendulum can silently tell me what terminology would be acceptable to my client. Therefore I may gently suggest such words as Universal Energy Field, Divine Energy, Universal Mind, Cosmic Mind, Gaia, The Earth Mother, God, etcetera. I don't have a problem with any of that, but, this I will say, there is not a nation or tribe anywhere in the world, no matter how remote, that does not have a belief system in some power higher than themselves.

I first introduced the word, "Guide" in Chapter Three, and said that I preferred to personify the information intermediary, because it made it easier to relate to. We often refer to the pendulum telling us something, while, more correctly, it is our guide telling us something , through the medium of the pendulum. Occasionally, by means of the pendulum, we may get an indication of who the Guide is, and they may well have been at one time in incarnation.

They would certainly be evolved spiritually, and have skills appropriate to the work in hand, which is why, from time to time, they change.

When we move on to the next level, after passing through the doorway called "Death", we may choose, if we have a well-developed gift, to use it still. What could be more loving than that we work with someone on Earth who needs our ministrations, and is open and accepting of what we have to offer?

Unfortunately there is a down side to this. The healer is open to the guide because he or she is working with an open heart and mind, but if someone is open to a discarnate being through abuse of himself or others, through such things, for example, as addiction to sex, drugs, alcohol, or the like, then you will see that they could be invaded by discarnate beings of a very different persuasion! When we leave the earth plain we take with us our character and personality. If we had bad habits while on earth, we have them still, until we decide to work on ourselves and make changes. If we were addictive in personality we still are faced with our problem. We deal with all these things in our own good time. We can receive help and support on this plane of course, but only if we seek it. On the next plane we are encouraged to go to school. Addictions play on character weaknesses. We need to get a grip on ourselves and take responsibility. Often it is addiction that is the problem, and we can be addicted to all sorts of things, food, shopping or computers for instance. There is a whole world out there, brought right into our home. Are we using this wonderful invention for Light or Dark purposes? And once our energy is open, how can we regulate the quality of the energy working with us?

This brings me to the reason for the need of a guardian of your channel. As I've said, good dowsing is all about impeccability, the limiting of the possibility for error. The guardian will filter what information is trying to come through to you, and hold negative influences at bay like a fire wall in a computer. We ourselves also have a responsibility to live our lives honourably and stay close to spiritual influences, whatever our persuasion. This is not necessarily about going to a particular place of worship. I much prefer the word Spirituality than the word Religion. Many evil acts have been perpetrated in the name of Religion, but Spirituality represents to me our *journey* through this world. I am much more interested in actions than in words. Words can come cheap, but actions always require effort. Watch what people do, not what they say.

So how do we go about choosing this all important Guardian of the Channel? They must be some one already on the other side of life, and they must be linked to you in love. They are often someone we have known, and who is known to have known us in their lifetime, but they could also be a member of our family who died before we were born, because, of course, they could still know and love us from the other side of life. They could also be someone who belongs more to your emotional family than your physical family, for example, a friend of yours or even a friend of one of your family whom you think would hardly have known you in life. The all important link is Love. Do remember, however, that you must establish that the person you choose is willing to do the job! In order to so this, use the simple Yes/No cross, or, better still the Truth Line. If this feels like too important a question to be asking so early on, just continue to play with the different crosses a little longer, until you feel more positive.

As it is important that you know that your guardian is in place, before you start asking **really important** questions, you need to establish a special little code between you, rather like an STD code on a telephone call.

When you start dowsing you only have a limited language of movements to choose from, but as you get more experienced and the language extends you could upgrade the code to something more complicated if you so chose. For example, in the early days you might choose the horizontal axis as your code. That would be a good one to use because it stands for personal relationships and the link with the material world.

So, right at the beginning, before you do anything else, you ask if the guardian of your channel is in place, and if you had chosen the horizontal line as your code, you would expect your pendulum to swing in that way, from side to side.

Now, a little tip for beginners – It *is* alright to amplify the movement of the pendulum a little in the early days of your practise. If you knock the pendulum a little, carefully, you will not be likely to change its direction, merely the force with which it moves. Remember, it's learning and you're learning. Its a bit like training a puppy. You have to show it what to do! I love to play the tenor recorder, and when I bought a new one, my teacher said to me, you need to train it. You see it is used to being a piece of wood, and now it has to learn to be a recorder!

Now, there are dowsers and there are good dowsers, and you, I'm sure, will want to be in the second group. Therefore there are five questions that you need to ask before you begin the Dowsing Exercise Proper. If this feels like a rigmarole, try to be patient a little longer.

Soon you will be able to simply pick up your pendulum and get on with the job, like me, but, as a beginner, you need to go through all the procedures in order to establish good practice and receive accurate information.

First think of a question to ask. Remember that in the early stages of your practice, it is a good idea to ask a question to which you already know the answer. Then go through the following procedure.

1. Is my guide in place?
2. Can I ask this question? (Meaning do I have the ability to ask this question?)
3. May I ask this question? (Meaning am I permitted to ask this question?)
4. Am I ready to ask this question? (Timing is important. Meaning is it the right time to ask this question?)
5. Is the question understood by my guide? (Remember the guide, at this stage

is probably learning too!)

If you get even one "NO" to any of these questions, wait. After a few moments, try again. If you still get a "NO" to any of the five questions, go back to practising the four crosses, and try the questions again another day.

One last piece of advice, to practise little and often is good. Don't try to achieve too much at any one time. A short practice every day works better than one big practice once a week! Believe me, I've done a lot of music practice over the years and I know!

To round off this chapter I would like to expand a point I mentioned very briefly earlier. I was speaking about our Guides and why they change from time to time. I said then that our Guides needed to be evolved spiritually and have skills appropriate to the work in hand. You will be able to understand that a different **Healing** Guide may be working with me when my client is suffering from, say arthritis, than when I'm working with autism. Guides work of course with our personal experiences and the amount of work and effort we have put in. Remember the old adage, God helps those who help themselves. For example if you have read and studied crystals quite a lot, if you feel linked to them, responsive to them, love and enjoy them, then your intuitive response to them is likely to be stronger. Also, there may be, as it were, a Senior Guide changeover as I pass through a new initiatory process of spiritual development. In other words, as I am permitted to work with more complex aspects of Healing, I am assigned a more evolved over-all guide to work with. It is, as we say:

"As above, so below"; as we ourselves evolve, we are matched with a more evolved guide on the other side of life, but the Guardian of the channel is likely to remain the same.

Chapter Eight

Talking about Chakras – Working with Colour

THE KUNDALINI EXPERIENCE

The divine power,
Kundalini shines
like the stem of a young lotus;
like a snake, coiled round upon herself.
she holds her tail in her mouth
and lies resting half asleep
at the base of the body.

Yoga Kundalini Upanishad (1.82)

Chakra is a Sanskrit word, meaning Wheel. We have inherited the energy system of chakras and their colours from the East, from ancient Yoga and Chinese Medicine. They are vortexes of energy, spinning on their own axes, and their purpose, when functioning properly, is clearing both negative energy patterns and resistance to change. Of course, just because information concerning chakras came, originally, from the East, it doesn't mean we in the West don't have them! We *all* have them. The simplest form of chakra system used consists of seven chakras, based on the seven different colours of the rainbow: Red, Orange, Yellow, Green or Pink, Blue, Indigo, Violet, which in combination make the white light of Enlightenment.

There are in fact many chakras in the body, and in my own work I have found it useful to extend this basic range a little. I work with twelve chakras, eight within the body and four above the head. The four above the head are for advanced work only, but I will discuss them, so that you are aware of their existence. The extra chakra within the body is between Blue and Green. It is a mixture of the two colours and is represented by Turquoise. The colours above the head are Magenta, White, Silver, and Gold.

Chakras are traditionally represented by lotus flowers, not unlike water lilies, growing in the mud, but flowering in the sun and, as they are wheels, they may spin too fast, too slow or at just the right speed. They represent the human condition, of an onward and upward journey towards Maturity and the Light. They can, like flowers, be closed, in bud, opening or in full flower, and as our personal development advances, each one in turn blossoms. When we are in full flower as it were, we are mature, fully evolved, authentic.

There is an energy, known as the Kundalini, represented by a curled-up snake, which lies dormant at the base of the spine, awaiting our awakening to a sense of self. As we become more aware in Life, it moves further and further up the spine, arousing the energy characteristics of each chakra in turn. Qualities start manifesting spontaneously, and express themselves in our lives, until, if we remain on the positive path of Light, we eventually achieve Enlightenment.

Years ago, my husband and I were in Athens, visiting the Acropolis. We wanted to employ an English-speaking guide. We were introduced to a lovely lady who was an archaeologist and a writer. She had just finished writing a book on Snake Energy, and she was the perfect guide for us that day. As it was only about ten o'clock in the morning, not too many other people were around and so we could go at a leisurely pace. She was interested to know that I was born in the Chinese Year of the Snake, and pointed out the things I was wearing whose design was linked to the snake. For instance I had diagonal crosses on the sides of my sunglasses. I was wearing flat silver coils in my ears, and my gold and silver bangle was marked with patterns derived from the snake. These things had all been chosen unconsciously by me, but probably with the aid of the pendulum! She pointed out that the decorative frieze at the top of the Parthenon building, at least in her mind, refers to the protective energy of Snake. In the museum on the Acropolis there are wonderfully patterned remains in red, black and ochre, of a statue, which consists of two huge coupling snakes, twisted together. I found them so interesting that I made a quick sketch of them, often so much more rewarding than taking a photograph. The statue reminded me of the Caduceus, the symbol for healing, which has two snakes entwined around a vertical staff, the staff of winged Mercury, messenger of the gods.

Our guide that day had a problem with her eyes, and I remember I gave her some healing there on the Acropolis, with the beautiful Temple of Athena in the background. Finally it was time to say our farewells, whereupon, while still facing me and looking intently at me, she made a fist at the bottom of my back. She then moved her fist up my spine, right up to the top of my head, saying, "The snake he go right up the back, right up the back, and when he get to the top of the head, the Buddha he smile". I was intrigued with this, particularly as I knew nothing about the snake energy, and had never heard of the Kundalini, at that time.

As if this wasn't extraordinary enough, when we arrived back home the very first person who came for Healing happened to be a clairvoyant and clairaudient. (One who sees and hears.) She had been to see me once before, but this time she brought a parcel, and she was obviously very excited about it. She said that the parcel was a present from my daughter who is in Spirit. She described my daughter, who had awoken her in the night, saying, "Heather Bray, Heather Bray", repeatedly in her ear. She was asked by my daughter to bring me a Buddha, the plump, seated, *smiling* one. She was told this would be what I would wish most of all to have, but my daughter was very particular in her request. The Buddha must be gold in colour and dressed in a white robe, and so this lady had been to the trouble of having my Buddha especially made for me. It was several years later, while on a home visit for Healing, that I was told the significance of the White Buddha. He is the Buddha of Compassion, the gold colour representing Divine Energy. Buddhas are often gold, and sometimes revered by devotees by overlaying the statues with gold leaf, that can becomes so thick, the original features of the statues are lost. I am not a Buddhist, but I have great respect for them, and I am sure that there are many elements of Buddhism in the work that I do.

Life is like a game of Snakes and Ladders, sometimes up a ladder, sometimes down a Snake. In a way, this imagery is back to front. Considering the Kundalini, it should be up the snake and falling down off the ladder. There are many, many ways of "falling off the ladder". It reminds me of Humpty Dumpy, who didn't fall off a ladder, but off a wall.

Humpty Dumpy sat on a wall.
Humpty Dumpy had a great fall.
All the King's horses and all the King's Men
Couldn't put Humpty together again.

Why not? He was only an egg. He had not evolved. I suspect there was insufficient personal involvement by this unevolved personality in his own healing. Too many people give away their personal power to others, expecting someone else to sort their lives out for them, and put them back together again. We go to doctors, thinking that they can sort our medical problems out, and of course they often do, but they work with secondary emanation, disease, (dis-ease made manifest) and treat from a selection of standard chemical drugs. Instead I and others like me are reaching and treating the primary, underlying states of mind, often preventing disease occurring, making disease less severe or preventing further exacerbation of disease. The method of treatment is different also, because instead of selecting from a standard list of chemical drugs, it is possible to treat with a careful, insightful selection of tinctures made directly from natural plant materials, relatively cheaply produced and with no harmful side effects, put together specifically for that individual at that particular time in their lives. The next time they visit, the remedies with which that particular person with that particular physical disease is treated will have changed, because their actual states of mind have adapted and improved. Mind has a huge influence on matter and every health problem I've ever come across has been affected positively or negatively by the person's state of mind. Healing by the methods that I and many like me use, helps people achieve improved attitudes and states of mind as well as getting back their sense of personal power. It is shown to them, through careful selection of the Bach Flowers, crystals, chakra colours, and what those things mean, where strengths and weaknesses lie, and what areas of the personality needs to be strengthened. Many people have the ability to work on these issues once they become aware of them.

We all need to take some responsibility for our own well-being, and realise that there's no change without a willingness to *change*. Sounds obvious doesn't it? We must first realise that we have a problem, that we may need help with our problem, and then have the courage and humility to be able to ask for that help. We remain at each Staging Post or Chakra of personal development both Here and Hereafter, until we, ourselves, are ready to make the changes necessary to move on up the ladder (or back on the wall!)

Halos, often in the colours of white, silver, or gold, expressing enlightenment, are depicted around the heads of Saints in spiritual paintings. The tradition is that their auras glowed in this way, because of their high level of spiritual development. Not everyone has the ability to see auras, but they are easier to see around the head of a person, when the background is plain and the light is not too bright. They are closely linked with the chakra system, in terms of colour. As a basic rule of thumb, those Light Colours tinged with white represent health and well-being, while those tinged with black or brown represent disharmony and illness. I have occasionally seen auras. The colours are like neon lights, but even more intense, and they appear to glow, standing out at a distance, just like a halo, from the person's profile. They could be any of the rainbow colours mentioned in this chapter.

I have never looked for these emanations, they have just suddenly, to my surprise, been there, but if you *do* start looking, you may well see them. They are also made visible in Kirlian photography, a photographic technique which reveals the energy emanated by physical forms. Children are often more in touch with such things than grown-ups. It would be good to get back to that simple, childlike open-minded sense of wonder and acceptance, trusting that The Infinite Divine Energy simply **is**. After all the evidence is all around us in Nature for those with eyes to see, and the idea that living cells, whether human, animal or plant radiate a presence in this way, is an enduring concept.

One thing for sure, while we are in this dimension we will always need to take some things on trust, because there is no way that we can work the whole thing out!

Here is a Bible quote. Matthew 18 verse 3. New International Version

And he said: "I tell you the truth, unless you change and become like little children, you will never enter the kingdom of heaven."

The only other chakras I would like to mention are those in the palms of both hands. They are Healing chakras, once again circular, and about four and a half centimetres across. Some of you, when you start 'Hands on' healing, may be made very aware of their presence. When I started healing first of all, I would be aware, for about two hours afterwards, of a radiant energy in the chakras of both hands, the healing energy having passed through my right hand, while my pendulum, held in my left hand, passed me information. The effect was very like the pleasant afterglow of spending time in the sun.

Talking of Healing Hands, here is another personal account. One night several years ago I had what is called a lucid dream. I was just on the very edge of sleep, a place where contact with the fourth dimension is very close. My elder daughter who died came to me in my Healing Room. I was absolutely delighted to see her of course. She said that she had something to show me. Sitting beside me on the small bed I use as a healing couch, she held up her left hand, fingers outstretched, with the palm towards me. What I saw amazed me because I could see right through the shape of her upheld hand and, instead of its usual characteristics, I saw a bright white sky and fluffy pale mauve clouds. She then got me to hold up my right hand, (my pendulum hand) with my palm facing her palm. She was able to show me that my hand was a mirror image of hers, complete with bright white sky and fluffy pale mauve clouds! She didn't speak about it, but I can only think it meant that we reflect each other and send each other messages across the Divide which exists between this world and the next. Finally, the doorbell rang. My husband answered it and in came a Quaker friend of ours. My daughter heard her coming down the hall and said, " If she's coming I'll have to go." and so we said hasty farewells and my daughter was gone, out through the kitchen door to the garden and away, whereupon I was immediately aware of being once more in our bedroom and wide awake.

TABULATION OF THE CHAKRAS I USE IN MY HEALING WORK

I shall discuss these in some detail because I think it is most useful, both in terms of self help healing and colour therapy, to have such information all in one place.

THE FOUR PETALLED LOTUS - The Root Chakra

The first chakra is the MULADHARA, which means root or support. It represents the life force and the will to survive. Its colour is red, the associated sense is smell and its position is between the anus and the genitals. However, remember that it also protects the body right down to the soles of the feet, psychologically and literally grounding us, and helping us heal our roots. The glandular connection is with the adrenals and the production of adrenaline, the hormone for "fight or flight ". Associated body parts are feet, legs, bones and large intestine, while malfunctions are obesity, haemorrhoids, constipation and sciatica. The connection is with the earth, the tribe, the family, family attitudes, genetic inheritance and physical survival needs. If we are functioning well here, we would be grounded and healthy, a good provider, physically and emotionally, both of our own needs and the needs of those in our family group. If we are under energised here, we are emotionally needy, with low self esteem. We may also live in a 'daydream', or be physically lethargic. When this chakra spins too fast we are over energised, and may be aggressive, bullying or self centred.

THE SIX PETALLED LOTUS – The Sacral Chakra

The second Chakra is the SVADISHISTHANA, meaning " One's own abode" or "sweetness." It is concerned with how we feel about our home and ourselves. The questions are, 'Am I happy with my home? Do I feel happy with myself?' The colour is Orange, the associated sense is taste, and its position is in the lower abdomen, between the navel and the genitals. This chakra is linked to the sacral nerve plexus (network), and so to the central nervous system. The relative glands are the ovaries and testes, and its physical links are with circulation, the kidneys, ovaries, testes, sex organs, bladder, prostate and womb. Malfunctions could be linked to any of these organs, and include impotence and frigidity. This chakra is about emotional balance. If it is over energised, spins too fast, we become manipulative, emotionally imbalanced, or possibly, sexually addictive. If on the other hand, it spins too slowly, or not at all, we may be frigid or impotent, over sensitive, or hard on ourselves. When this chakra spins at the correct speed, we are trusting and expressive, in touch with our own feelings and creative. Our sexual energy brings a sense of completeness and integration.

THE TEN PETALLED LOTUS –The Solar Plexus Chakra

The third chakra is the MANIPURA, meaning Lustrous Gem, or City of Jewels, also known as the solar plexus, linking it to the sun. Its position is between the navel and the base of the sternum or breastbone. The glandular link is with the pancreas and the sensual link is sight. It is connected to intense feelings such as laughter, joy and anger. Malfunctions are ulcers, diabetes, eating disorders such as anorexia and bulimia and hypoglycaemia (abnormal reduction of the sugar content of the blood). The colour here is yellow and the main issues are personal power, sense of self, spiritual connectedness and discrimination. Ego means "I am" in Latin. Ego is not wrong. We need to establish a sense of who we are, and find our place in the world, but eventually, material possessions and even most personal relationships are not sufficiently fulfilling, and so we come to the challenge of the change of direction, what in Greek is called the Metanoia. It is the place of repentance, the time of reflection and regret for what has happened, and we start to rethink the whole thing. What have we been overlooking? Why do we not feel happier? If we are lucky enough to have a car, we may think we would feel better with a bigger one, a better one, a newer one, and, just for a little while, satisfying the desire works, but only for a little while! We can be addicted to many things and one is spending money. Maybe if we had several cars, we could be happy. I'm afraid once you go down that road of feeling you don't have enough of anything, then you'll never have enough. What matters in the end is not what you *possess*, but what you are like as a person. That is our most valuable asset, rich or poor. Of *course* it's not wrong to have money. Money often comes as a result of being good at what you do. It's an energy, like any other, and should be respected as such, but there is also a responsibility to use it sensibly, not squander it and certainly not to borrow beyond your means to repay.

Do we know ourselves? Do we now know what and who is important to us? If we are too self important, we become controlling, judgemental and superior. This is what happens when this chakra spins too fast. If it doesn't spin fast enough we are insecure and too concerned with what others might think, often trying to prop ourselves up with over spending on material goods, to try to produce what we think of as a good self image, that will make others respect and like us. Actions such as these are fear based, and we often use the expression "yellow " or "lily-**livered**", to describe cowardice. And what is a coward if not someone who is afraid to be seen as they really are? If, on the other hand, this chakra is balanced, we may have insights, (the link is with both outer and inner sight.) which set us on the spiritual path. We recognise our personal power, but do not flaunt it, and are spontaneous and uninhibited. The solar plexus is a potential battleground between the soul and the ego. It is basically a case of more Ego less Soul and more Soul less Ego. In many ancient cultures the sun was worshipped as a god, a recognition that we ourselves are not the centre of life on earth, that there is indeed a higher power. Here the lesson is respect both for ourselves and others: for who we, or they, are, and not what we ourselves, or they, have. The relative body parts are the digestive system, including the stomach, pancreas, and liver, and the muscles. Disfunctions may be such things as stomach ulcers, diabetes or allergies.

THE TWELVE PETALLED LOTUS - The Heart Chakra

This is the ANAHATA or Heart chakra. Its name means the sound created without two things striking, therefore " *Unstruck* ". This is fascinating when considering the texts which try to explain how the whole universe started evolving. In the Bible it says that in the beginning was the Word. What word? What sound? If there was nothing else in existence there would be nothing for it to "strike" against, but that doesn't mean that sound was not possible purely as an emanation from the Absolute.

This is the Heart Chakra, the seat of Love and Wisdom and as such is the bridge between the lower triad (group of three) of chakras, concerned with matter, and the upper triad, concerned with Spirit. The Anahata contains two intersecting triangles that make up a six-pointed star, demonstrating the perfect balance between the downward pointing Spirit descending towards Matter and the upward pointing Matter rising towards Spirit.

Here is an interesting quote from the magazine "Living Lightly". This is from an article written by Virginia Kennedy, entitled, "The Intelligence of the Heart".

"Over the past twenty years scientists have discovered new information about the heart revealing that it is much more complex than originally thought. There is scientific evidence that the heart sends us emotional and intuitive signals to help us govern our lives. So the phrase, "I'm following my heart" appears to have physiological justification."

This suggests that the heart is not merely an organ for pumping blood around the body, but that it has a deeper purpose, linked to the mind and the intelligence. Our mind links us to Cosmic Mind and differs from the brain, which of course ceases to function at bodily death. The mind however, because it does not depend on our physical body, but is linked to and is supported by our permanent Light Body, continues to function in the normal way. In fact the mind, which is always linked to Cosmic Mind is carried forward by us from the beginning of our Soul Time to the present day and the wisdom stored there can be accessed through holistic medicine methods; the linking of Body Mind and Spirit. Also of course the memories held in the Mind are passed to our minds when Past Life Recall is made possible by means of a paradigm (an example) shift of personal consciousness.

The colours here are both green and pink, green for male energy and pink for female energy. However, if you were treating a female for problems concerning a male or her own male side you might well use green, and correspondingly use pink with a male. Also, as we all carry both male and female attributes, it is not always possible to ascertain, from appearances, which is predominant. Therefore, we may need to resort to the pendulum in the matter.

When we are balanced, and the chakra is spinning at the correct speed, we are compassionate towards all sentient (feeling) beings, **including ourselves**. That can often be the toughest challenge of all! Compassion means literally, to feel someone's pain with them. When we are able to be truly compassionate it usually means that we have experienced some often considerable pain ourselves. In fact the heart has been, as we say, broken, not broken as in beyond repair, but broken open, so that, thereafter, we work with an open heart. Our basis for love is then broader based and more unconditional, with people outside our family circle becoming like brothers and sisters to us.

A quote from Albert Einstein published in the New York *Post,* November 28th, 1972. " A human being is part of the whole, called by us the "Universe," a part limited in time and space. He experiences himself, his thoughts and feelings as something separated from the rest - a kind of optical delusion of his consciousness. This delusion is a kind of prison for us, restricting us to our personal desires and to affection for a few persons nearest to us. Our task must be to free ourselves from this prison by widening our circle of compassion to embrace all living creatures and the whole of nature in its beauty. Nobody is able to achieve this completely, but the striving for such achievement is in itself part of the liberation and a foundation for inner security. "

When tragedy strikes we often shut down in the area of the heart for a while because everything is too painful to endure. We talk of being downhearted. I know from personal experience that this can actually happen. A few months after our daughter died I was in Quaker Meeting and all of a sudden there was a great leap in my chest. I literally felt my heart chakra jump back into its rightful position once again!

If badly hurt by someone, we may think that we will never let anyone do this to us ever again. I use the metaphor of the hedgehog, curled up and extremely vulnerable, in the middle of a busy road, unable to move. It is only later that we hopefully will realise that to shut ourselves off from the energy of love is to shut ourselves off from life itself. Be brave enough to live, love, and risk losing and feeling the pain of that all over again. It's worth the risk.

Physical problems may be high blood pressure, heart disease, asthma or even lung cancer. These things may come about if the heart has had to endure long periods of unresolved stress, unhappiness, or subjugation of our will to the will of another. The associated body parts are the heart, the chest, arms, hands, lungs and circulation. The sense is touch. Malfunctions are asthma, blood pressure, heart disease and lung disease. When the chakra spins too fast we can be possessive or co-dependent. We can withhold emotionally in order to punish, make our love conditional or very dramatic. When spinning too slowly, or not at all, we fear rejection, are self-pitying, or feel unworthy of love. As I've said before, when the heart is open our basis for love is much broader, and we are more likely to be able to love unconditionally. The glandular connection is said to be with the thymus, but I prefer to treat the thymus separately, and give the heart/mind a status of its own.

THE THYMUS

As stated above, some people would combine this next chakra with the heart, but I like to think of it separately. It is too important a chakra to be combined with another. It is the Thymus, halfway between the throat and the heart. The colour is Turquoise, used for psychic protection in many cultures, and very much linked to protection in the body, as it is concerned with the immune system, helping to fight infection. The famous scientist, Louis Pasteur is reported to have said on his deathbed, " I got it wrong." Disease, he realised, is not so much about bacteria as about the different effects they have on different people. Some are vulnerable while others in the same group remain unaffected.

Interestingly the thymus is also said to be linked to the Angelic Realms and their protection on a spiritual level. There is a strong belief among many people, myself included, that we each have a Guardian Angel. There is an excellent little book, called," Who is my Guardian Angel?" by Veronique Jarry, that devotes a particular angel to every four or five days around the year, according to your day and month of birth. Many have been helped by this book, and it is amazing how the qualities of the appropriate angel are reflected in the person. Another excellent book on Guardian Angels is "Angel signs - a celestial guide to the powers of our own guardian angel." (See bibliography at the end of book for all book reference details)

THE SIXTEEN PETALLED LOTUS - The Throat Chakra

This is the VISHUDDI, which means purification. Its associated colour is blue and its position is central, at the base of the neck. The connection is with the thyroid gland and parathyroid glands, which are four pea-like bodies, embedded in the lobes of the thyroid, an upper and a lower on each side. They are ductless glands controlling the utilisation of calcium, and their over action causes rarefaction of the skeleton and spontaneous fractures. The thyroid itself controls the rate of body metabolism and the general cycle of building up and breaking down of body tissues. The senses linked to this chakra are sound and hearing. The associated body parts are the throat, ears, mouth, teeth, nose and neck. Malfunctions are sore throat, swollen glands, colds and thyroid problems. Its connection is with synthesis, (bringing things together, making a whole out of) gathering things together in preparation for the special disciplines required for promoting the gift of inner sight. Here we recognise how we truly feel and gain the confidence to communicate those emotions to others. If this chakra is too open, we may be arrogant, dogmatic, over-talkative or self-righteous. If it spins sluggishly or not at all, we hold back from self expression, feeling that we will not be heard or that what we say would somehow initiate conflict. This in fact may be true, but we still need to *express* and not *suppress* our emotions, because this is the very thing that causes the blockages in the energetic , or Chi system in the body. Also sometimes there are things that the other person *needs* to hear.

Sometimes I encourage my client to send a card or write a letter to the person or persons concerned, because you can then take time to present things exactly how *you* wish, without the other person interrupting or drawing you into saying more than you intend to. If, once the letter is written, you think it ill-advised to send it, then destroy it in some way, maybe by burning, burying or tearing it up. Most importantly, don't reread it because that tends to reprogram the information it contains back into your brain, and your aim is to get it out and away. Don't think either, "Oh I'll probably never send it , so why bother to write it?" It really does matter that you express yourself, that you take the time and trouble to put your feelings into words.

It's also good to talk about the problem, provided you know the listener can be trusted with the information. Over the years I have been privileged to hear many things. My clients can tell me *anything,* knowing I will not be judgemental, nor will it be repeated to anyone else. Plenty of time is allowed for talking. This is why the healing session of two hours divides roughly into one and a half hours or so for going through the remedies and discussion, while the last half to three quarters of an hour is devoted to Hand-On Healing. Occasionally during the Healing, I have found a chakra blockage which will not shift. The method I use is to lay a selected crystal on the body at the particular point of blockage, to act as a "keyhole" for the Healing Energy The crystal is then covered by my left hand on order to initiate delivery of the healing energy, but more of this later in Chapter Nine. I need to tell my client that I've found a resistant energy and enquire of them What's going on? What are you holding back? What have we not discussed to do with this chakra? There has always been something, consciously or unconsciously held back, but once the problem is spoken about, the energy blockage clears immediately, and I am then able to go forward and complete the healing, showing how important it is to express emotion and not suppress it. When this chakra spins at the correct speed we communicate well, and are artistically inspired.

Note that chakras go *through* the body, they don't just "sit" on the surface, and so, in a way, they have a front and a back. There are a lot of very creative people living in Cornwall and sometimes they get "blocked" in their field of self expression. When someone comes to me with this kind of problem, the first place I would look for congested energy would be the back of the neck. The front of the neck is concerned with communication, and the back of the neck with creativity. Creativity is *so important* to our well-being. It is linked to originality and the element of play. It brings us closer to an understanding of the Divine in that we become as little gods in one area of our lives. We get to choose what *we* want to bring into existence, and so bring about an expansion of consciousness, which can then be assimilated and enjoyed by others.

THE LOTUS WITH TWO LARGE PETALS
one on either side of a central circle
containing a downward pointing triangle- The third eye

This is the AJNA, meaning to know, to perceive or to command. The associated colour is Indigo, which is mid way between royal blue and navy blue. Its function is direct perception and the inner state is self mastery. In fact the symbol for the Ajna looks rather like an eye. This chakra is referred to as the Third Eye, and lies above the eyebrows and between the eyes. The associated body parts are the eyes, the base of the skull and the Cerebellum, or ancient brain. It is concerned with the ability to see with other than the physical eyes.

William James wrote in, " Varieties of Religious Experience ", (New York : New American Library, 1958.) - ".....our normal waking consciousness, rational consciousness as we call it, is but one special type of consciousness, whilst all about it, parted from it by the filmiest of screens, there lie potential forms of consciousness entirely different..........No account of the universe in its totality can be final which leaves these other forms of consciousness quite disregarded"

The Ajna is concerned with transcending the physical world in order to tap into limitless knowledge, which can be directly accessed by those who are sufficiently spiritually evolved, *without the need to go to an intermediary.* In other words this chakra is associated with enlightenment and wisdom. The glandular link is with the pituitary, which has sometimes been described as the leader of the endocrine orchestra, because it controls the activity of the other glands to some extent. It is a tiny gland the size of a pea. It occupies a little socket between the right and left middle cranial fossae, behind the crossing of the optic nerves. The sense is that known as the sixth sense or intuition. Physical disfunctions you need to look for are headaches, poor vision, neurological disturbances and glaucoma, whereas emotional disfunctions might be such things as nightmares, hallucinations or schizophrenia.

If this chakra spins too fast the person may be arrogant, highly logical to the detriment of their intuition, or dogmatic. If it spins too slowly or not at all, they may not be prepared to work sufficiently at their gift to ensure that it develops and grows. When this chakra is balanced and spinning correctly the person will be highly intuitive and be using the gift wisely, to the best of their ability. They will experience unusual phenomena but be able to take them in their stride, taking a balanced viewpoint. The important operative words here are LOVE and RESPECT. Problems occur in dealing with unusual phenomena when people or entities on this side or the other side of life are not sufficiently LOVED AND RESPECTED. I have had a lot of experience in dealing with so-called unusual phenomena and I cannot express this last point too strongly. I see in the media that sometimes things are very badly mishandled. There is exploitation for power and monitory gain in this area as in many others and those concerned, maybe unknowingly, put themselves and others in potentially serious danger.

THE THOUSAND PETALLED LOTUS – The Crown Chakra.

This is the SAHASRARA, meaning thousand fold. The associated colour is violet and the position is the top or crown of the head. It is often referred to as the Crown Chakra. Its function is union, and the malfunction is alienation. Please remember that this is the Spirit's point of entry in the developing foetus and also the highest orifice for departure of the Spirit at death. As such, it can be an extremely delicate point for healing and should not be physically touched during healing unless you are accomplished as a Healer.

I would like to mention here something called the Escaton, which concerns perfect alignment and unity, illustrated by the statement, " I am in my Father and you are in me and I am in you." This is the Healing state. The Minister of Healing, is, as it were in the gap between the Divine Creator and the Healee. The Healer and the Healee, at the point of healing, are as one, and that One is at one with the Divine Energy, in perfect alignment. In other words there is only the One. Because of this perfect alignment and unity, it is in no way surprising that information and assistance can flow from one part of "The Body" to "Another" with consummate ease.

The associated body parts are the skin, the upper skull and the **right** and **left brain**, as seen looking down on the top of a person's head from behind. **left brain** controls the right side of the body and **right brain** controls the left side. The related sense is beyond the self and the glandular link is with the pineal, meaning 'shaped like a pine-cone', which is interesting when you think of the image of the thousand petalled lotus skullcap. Its real function remains a mystery. In birds it seems to be linked to their ability to navigate using the available light as a reference, so in a sense to see in the dark, for there seems to be little correlation between the amount of light available and what is visible. This brings to mind the Biblical psalm 139, vv 11 and 12.

"O Lord........If I say "Surely the darkness will hide me and the light become night around me," even the darkness will not be dark to you; the night will shine like the day, for darkness is as light to you."

Those who are sufficiently enlightened have been given the power to discover the dark energies, wherever they may be hiding and the ability to work alongside guides, in love and respect, to transform them.

Physical disfunctions are linked to sensitivity to pollution, chronic exhaustion, epilepsy and Alzheimer's Disease. Emotional disfunctions are associated with confusion, depression and obsessional thinking. When the chakra spins too fast the person may be psychotic or manic depressive, be frustrated or have a sense of unrealised power. If the chakra is spinning sluggishly or not at all the person could be constantly tired, very indecisive or maybe feels little or no no sense of belonging. This is not the same as feeling as many of us do, that this world is not our true home, that we are merely visiting. When this chakra is spinning at the correct speed, the person will be pretty much at peace with themselves, will have a magnetic personality, will be enlightened and will be able to achieve "miracles," and maybe even Miracles, for everyone's mutual benefit.

Now we come to the last four chakras that I wish to discuss. The only evidence I have for their existence is experiential. Their colours are Magenta, White, Silver and Gold.

Their positions are above the head. It is not possible to give you exact positions because they will vary according to the expansion or contraction of the person's aura. However they will always appear in the same order.

Magenta. This is the Energy of the Universal Archetypal Mother, and is the "Heavenly" aspect, or mirror image, of the Divine Earth Mother, linked of course to the Root Chakra and the colour Red. So we have come full circle. Magenta is another higher vibration of Red.

Next we have White, standing for Enlightenment, when all the previously mentioned colours of light are put together they form White Light, the Energy Representation of the Enlightened One.

And now we have Silver, which has long been associated with the Moon and the Divine Feminine Principle. A quote from the section on Silver, in the marvellous "bible" of crystals, "Love is in the Earth." "It (silver) provides for a very strong connection between the physical and astral bodies, assuring that one may always "come home" from the astral plane. It tends to strengthen the "silver cord" which connects the astral body to the physical body, providing for diminishment of the unconscious fear of the inability to return." Certainly when the Healee is ready and the Healer is sufficiently initiated, there can be visions, mystical experiences and Energy connections of a high order reached through this chakra.

Finally we come to Gold, which has long been associated with the Divine Masculine Principle, and the Sun. This is a link with the Ineffable, that which defies all description or definition. The Absolute. Only Faith, Trust and obedient Service can take us there.

These last four are only likely to be required to be used by people of considerable Healing expertise and experience.

Now for some associated stories.

A Root chakra story - A tale of India

To give you a real life illustration of the root chakra, let me tell you what happened to us several years ago. We were going on holiday abroad and were making our way to an airport in London. The train pulled in at Truro station and I noticed a particular man and woman, standing waiting on the platform. Because of the way they were dressed, I took them to be Indian. Remember this is Cornwall, and we don't see many obviously foreign nationals. My husband and I were already seated at a table for four people. However, there were two more seats that were vacant, but reserved. I just knew that these two people were destined to be our travelling companions, and so it turned out to be. My husband had taken a book with him to read on the train, a most interesting book in fact, called, "Answers" written by a young Indian Avatar, (the descendant of a Hindu Deity, in physical form.) called Mother Meera. When the young couple had sat down, I noticed the gentleman nod knowingly to his wife. They had obviously noticed the book. As we have travelled in India, we were soon engaged in conversation with the couple. They were actually both University Lecturers on a year's sabbatical. The wife was lecturing at an English university for a year and her husband had taken a year off to be with her and look after their young child, who was also with them. This trip to England had recently been foretold by the lady's uncle, who lived on the ashram where Mother Meera had been raised. That was an interesting and unexpected connection but there were more. The lady was wearing two rings with large stones in them, which had been given to her by this uncle. One had a red stone and the other an orange one. Before wearing these rings she had been very prone to falling over, hurting her feet and legs and since wearing them the accidents had stopped. Her uncle had told her always to wear them for protection. (Red for the root chakra and orange for the sacral chakra.)

A tale of special powers

Then an even stranger story was told, about how this uncle had acquired his special powers. When he was very young, about six years of age, he became very ill with a fever, so ill, in fact, that he was not expected to live. During the fever he started to speak with the voice of a much older male. The voice was recognised by his grandmother to be that of her dead husband. He spoke about a pot of money that he had buried in a secret place before his death, out in a certain field, away from the house. The family took the message seriously and went searching. Sure enough they found the hoard, just as described by the little boy! The child went on to recover, unharmed, from the fever, and to regain his normal voice, but from that day forward, he had special powers, particularly the gift of prophesy.

Now I want to speak a little about **your use of the pendulum** in work with chakras, either for yourself, or with permission, for someone else. Obviously it will tell you whether the chakra is spinning too fast, too slowly or just right by using the Yes/ No cross. Then, if you were working, for instance, on the Heart Chakra, you could discover whether the colour was pink or green,

Positions of Chakras and Colours

gold — 4th chakra above crown

silver — 3rd chakra above crown

white — 2nd chakra above crown

magenta — 1st chakra above crown

violet — crown — SAHASRARA

indigo — third eye — AJNA

blue — throat — VISHUDDI

turquoise — thymus — THYMUS

green/pink — heart — ANAHATA

yellow — solar plexus — MANIPURA

SVADISHISHANA

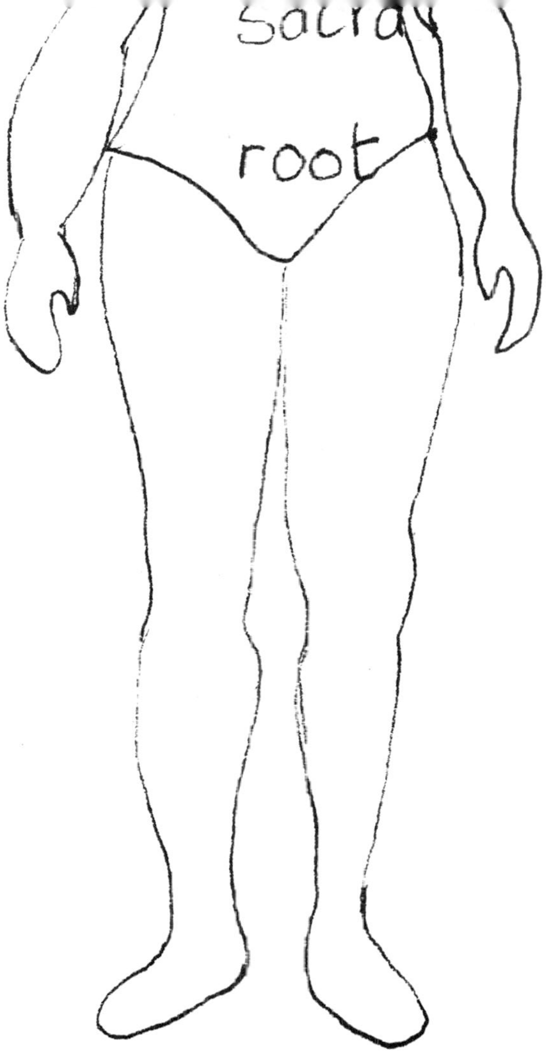

MULADHARA

orange

red

The colour red
protects from
the top of the
legs to the
soles of the feet.

sacral

root

by the same means, and then finally you could ask whether the colour was tinged with white or black, or was simply pure colour. As you become more proficient, of course you may be able to discern degrees of positivity and negativity, all the way from just into the positive right up to the forty five degree Truth Line position.   For example, is there a lot of white mixed in here or only a little? These three pieces of information, pieced together, would tell you quite a lot, and identify the areas in which work needs to be done.

When I use the term "work" , it doesn't mean dull and boring. If you need more of a certain colour in your aura, it would be lovely to find a special little place, maybe a small shelf or table which would not get disturbed, to gather various things in that colour, maybe a crystal, a candle, a postcard, some coloured water in a pretty bottle, beads, material, a plant, some shells....... I could go on and on. You may then find that you get attracted to a particular shade of your chosen colour. (Why not collect a few paint colour charts?) Something in you is responding naturally in this way for your own healing and well-being. I have noticed many times when working with colour that people will often come in wearing exactly the colour they need, or maybe they will say that they have just decorated a room in that colour. If we allow ourselves to be authentic, not wearing a "mask" or pretending, we can all be intuitive.

Working with colour

Sometimes, when a client has seen me for several sessions already, I may 'hear in my head' "Work with colour today" This is a very interesting way of working - insightful and enjoyable. When this happens I will know beforehand what colour the person needs. This is to do with lack of colour in their aura. I find what the colour is by working up through the nine main auric colours of the body itself - Red, Orange, Yellow, Green, Pink, Turquoise, Blue, Indigo, Violet. As I go through these in my head, the pendulum will go over on to the Truth Line on one of them. That colour which has been picked out is indicative of the chakra which needs working on, as illustrated at length above. I would put together a small group of articles in that colour, and light a coloured candle - I have a set of coloured glass candle jars and I light a small night light inside. I might also put a crystal and maybe a bit of cloth, a shell, a flower, alongside. Because the colour chosen will be the colour they need, I usually get an interesting response, and certainly their attention. Don't forget to also draw their attention to the afterimage colour, as shown in the tabulation overleaf. There are lots of good books on chakras and colour but two that I can recommend for this work are -

"Ambika's guide to healing and wholeness - the energetic path to the chakras and colour." This is a particularly amazing book, wonderfully insightful.

The other one, which is beautifully illustrated, is "The book of Chakra

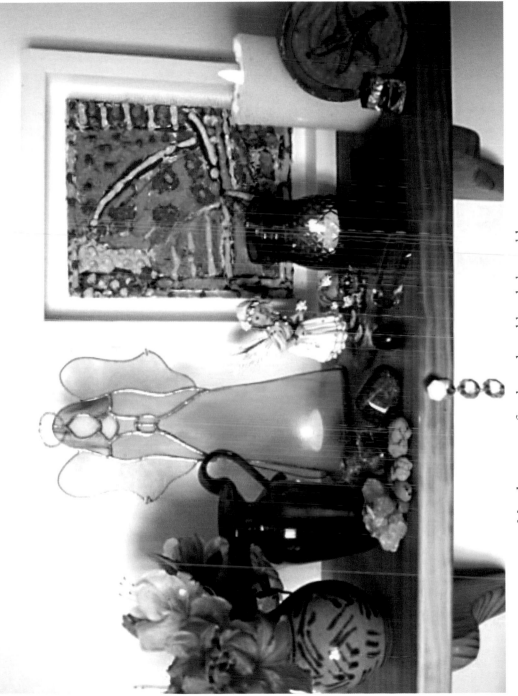

My altar set up for the colour blue, balanced by orange

Healing." by Liz Simpson.

Having been given the colour, you could use either, or both of these books, together with your pendulum to build an insightful and fruitful session with your client.

You will notice, in the illustration of my little altar, that I offset the colour **blue**, which is the main colour in this case, with the colour **orange**. This is because these two colours are **complimentary**. Colours work on balancing the brain, and the brain is composed of a right hemisphere and a left hemisphere. Therefore, when working with colour it is always important to remember what colour is complimentary to the main colour.

When working with light, this colour is known as the **after image**. To give you an example, if you stare at a bright red square of card (say about 25 cms square) placed on a white background for a minute or so in good natural light, you might begin to get a bright turquoise/blue light of a neon intensity beginning to appear in a band around the edges of the red square. This is known as the afterimage and is produced naturally in the brain. If after this time you remove the red square, you may well experience a square of turquoise/blue light on the white card, exactly where the red square was.

If you are interested to know more about healing with colour, refer to " Healing with Colour" by Theo Gimbal. See bibliography.

Here is a list of Chakra colours and their After image colours

Chakra Colour	After Image
Red	Turquoise/Blue
Orange	Dark Blue
Yellow	Violet
Green	Magenta
Turquoise/Blue	Red
Dark Blue	Orange
Violet	Yellow
Magenta	Green

You will recall, from the illustrated diagram on chakras, pages 82 and 83, that twelve colours, in all, are mentioned, including four above the head: magenta, white, silver and gold. These colours have an additional purpose, besides being linked to the vortexes, or energy centres, for healing. When I have finished my negative energy clearing work, working stage by stage, **up** through the body, sometimes continuing up beyond the head, I may be led to ask whether I should bring a particular colour right down through the body to the feet. I would get a Yes or No response to this question. If the response was Yes, I would go through the list of colours, starting with Red, to see which colour it should be.

The appropriate colour is then visualised by the client, as coming **down** through the body, through every cell, fibre, muscle, organ and bone of the body, including down the arms to the fingers and beyond, and down the legs and feet and out through the toes and beyond, clearing out all negativity, and taking it away for transformation. It would be at this point that the affirmation, (as to where the healing energy came from,) would be made. This visualisation is something which can make your client feel wonderfully calm and peaceful, and is also something that they can continue to practice for themselves at home, while relaxing.

Note that the colour chosen will be one that you had used with your client in healing that day. In other words, if you had stopped at violet, the crown chakra, you would not be bringing magenta, white, silver or gold down through the body. Also note that whether or not you bring **colour** down through your client's body, always use your pendulum to help you track their **energy back** down to the soles of their feet once again, after healing. Also suggest that they get **carefully** off the bed and that they press the soles of their feet into the ground to re-establish their presence in the 'here and now.'

Also note that the pendulum gives me a forward, clockwise circle, (meaning, "Keep going,") if I am to continue up above and beyond violet, to one of the next four positions above the head, during healing, as not everyone is ready to take such powerful energy.

Whatever job you have been given by the Divine Energy, it is important that you are able to successfully and efficiently ground yourself afterwards. I have no special ritual for this, except to say a heartfelt, "Thank you," to those guides and helpers who have helped me see the job through. Then I simply come downstairs from my Healing Room, (It is important to have a special place for working, if that is at all possible, away from your normal living space,) and get on with the ordinary things of life, like preparing a meal, or seeing to the needs of our little dog. I don't take myself too seriously, and whatever marvellous and wonderful things have occurred, and there have been very many, I know that I have only been a small link in the long chain of Love.

Chapter Nine
Choosing, Cleansing and Storing Crystals

For those who love crystals it is very fascinating to go in search of something new to add to their collection. They are all so very special and beguiling and the choice can be almost overwhelming. You are also making an important decision because, providing you look after it, a crystal will last you your whole lifetime and be used time and time again, getting more and more powerful. Because of this I have drawn up a 'wish list' of those I think you would find most useful. They are a classic set that I would not like to be without. I have listed four different crystals in relation to each chakra, or vortex of energy within the body. This is not because you need all four, but in order to give you helpful insight on how to choose and build your collection. Note that the crystals do not have to be used together in their sets. All crystals are compatible with all others. They are totally interchangeable.

My initial advice would be to always buy from someone you feel is a pleasant helpful person, someone who would choose and display their stock carefully and have a love and respect for the crystals that they sell. The situation and atmosphere in which crystals have been displayed affects their energy, although the love and attention you give them once they are in your care can revive those which have been harvested or stored in a negative environment.

When there are several crystals of the same type to choose from, if possible pick up any one that you feel especially attracted to. Stroke it gently to wake it up, then holding the pendulum in one hand and the crystal in the other, see what you can discover about its energy. I would hope to see the pendulum swing on the Healing Line or maybe even describe the Working/Thinking Circle, if you are familiar with the second part of the pendulum protocol. If it is not yet doing either of these, blow gently on the front and back of the crystal. This is to cleanse the crystal and dislodge any negative energy which may have stagnated within it because of how or by whom it has been handled. If it still does not respond it would be best not to buy it, as it doesn't resonate with your energy and it is not for you. Sometimes special crystal specimens are shown in locked display cases. If this happens then it is possible to tune into one which is especially attracting your attention and access its energy through the glass. If you get an encouraging reading from your pendulum it is worth getting the case unlocked and going through the above procedure.

The practice of nudging a crystal awake, and blowing on it to cleanse it of negative energy when you have finished using it, should become part of your ritual every time you use a crystal in a Healing situation.

Once I get a crystal home I catalogue it so that I am quite clear what it is I have. It would also be useful to take a photograph of it to go alongside the name. If you do not have a method like this it is very easy to make mistakes and forget, as the collection grows, what the different crystals are and, although you are going to use them instinctively and not logically, there may be times when it is helpful to know their different properties, which is why I have made such an extensive tabulation at the end of this chapter.

Next I would hold my crystal under cold water in a large bowl, splashing the water over it freely, or running cold water into a sink, making sure that I first put the plug in the sink so that there is no risk of losing the precious crystal down the drain! Sounds obvious I know, but stranger things have happened! Having held it in the stream of clear water, imagining a beautiful waterfall, for a minute or two, I then dry it carefully on a clean cloth and place it on my little shelf which I designate as an altar, for several days, only taking it off if I want to hold it in order to get to know it and build a relationship between us. Remember it is a friend and working partner and you need to build a bond between you. You are going to be helping each other to perform sacred duties.

Crystals come out of the earth. That is their natural home and so I try to give them a home dedicated to them which feels right and natural to them. Because of this I have a large shallow box, with small sections in it, (actually an old box to hold letters, from a printer) each of which will hold two or three crystals. This box is where they live if they are not working. It is covered with a clean cloth in order to keep out the dust and also to protect them from too much light. Sometimes you may feel that you would like to put them in a sunny spot for a little while for some reason, maybe to help someone with healing from a distance. That is fine, but please do not leave them there for too long. If you want to leave crystals out please don't place them in the full heat of the sun and make sure to wash or dust them frequently, so that they look and feel at their best. They are alive with energy and need to be treated sympathetically.

When using crystals for healing do not be governed by rules, nor be limited because some book or other, including this one, tells you that a particular crystal is good for a particular ailment or emotion. These are guidelines only. If you feel that the information given is correct for you and your client in a particular circumstance, then follow it, but if your instinct is telling you something else, go with that. We are dealing primarily with emotions here. It is about having a ritual that you are *comfortable* with and also about what your intention is. If your *intention* for that person is genuinely to help them, then that will have an influence on the outcome, no matter how inexperienced your working practice is. You are not working with the illness here, but with the primary emotional energetic causes. Do not even follow the system on the next page for crystals as linked to the chakra system when it doesn't seem to feel right. I don't! If I get for example, a strong feeling that I should be using say turquoise for the feet and leg area, I check with my guides through the pendulum and, if I get confirmation through the truth/healing line then *that* is what I do. Healing is about being open attentive and watchful. You are an instrument of the Divine Energy not of somebody, anybody, who has written a book. Wisdom does not come out of books, it comes out of personal experience. Books simply confirm for you that which your heart already knows. For me it has always been about following my intuition: carefully following what my guides and nobody else are telling me, through the language of the pendulum. Books can help of course. By all means read what I have to say. It will give you confidence when you start, but I expect you, sooner or later, to feel the need to adapt what I tell you to your own way.

You are an individual. Take only what is helpful and proves to be useful to your Divine Purpose from what I, and others, freely offer.

Finally, sometimes you may feel that a particular crystal is needed but should not actually be placed on the body. Rather you feel you are being told by guides, that the crystal should be placed in a certain position alongside the body but at a distance from it. That's fine. Follow your intuition. Another time you may feel that a crystal should be in a certain position on the body but you cannot get it to stay there. In a situation such as this you can place the crystal in position, holding it there with your hand for a few seconds and mentally asking the person's body to take an energy reading of the crystal and remember it. Your can then quite happily place the crystal to one side.

STONES FOR THE ROOT CHAKRA

RED JASPER - bright brick red.
Red jasper is an excellent stone for 'Grounding' a person's energy. It is therefore connected to the root chakra. It is a stone of nurture bringing tranquility and wholeness, and has the energy, solidity and strength of Mother Earth. It is good for dream recall and shamanic journeying. It also has a practical energy in that it aids quick thinking and organisational abilities, helping one to be focussed. Through meditation it can provide insights for rectification of unjust situations and is generally known as a 'stone of health'. It strengthens the circulatory system and can help to restore tissue deterioration of the internal organs.
<u>Suggested placings</u> From the feet to the pelvis. The forehead.

GARNET - deep red or pink.
Garnet is good for clearing negative energy. It energises, revitalises and balances energy, bringing serenity. It is good at controlling anger, particularly of

oneself. Garnet is attuned to the heart energy and represents love. It therefore helps with self acceptance, and acceptance of the current situation as a starting point for mental and spiritual progress. It helps to regulate the controlled rise of the kundalini energy. Also it can help to activate other crystals by being placed alongside. It is good for purification, cleansing and elimination in the body. It can help bone problems, the heart and the blood. It can help in all aspects of regeneration both emotional and physical. The gentler energy of a pink garnet would be good to use, when working with someone who has a heart condition, not just in the area of the heart but within the root chakra also.

Suggested placings   From the feet to the pelvis. The heart.

HEMATITE - heavy, shiny metallic silver colour.

Hematite is shiny silver in colour when polished. It is excellent for grounding, balancing and realignment of energy. It also has a protective energy against psychic invasion. This stone aids concentration, focus and confidence as well as promoting original thought and enhancing memory. I use two or three crystals together to help mend broken bones or to realign energy, for example in the spine. It helps the bone 're-member' how it was before and to facilitate this you place one at the top, one in the middle and one at the lower end of the break, or the area needing realignment. It helps dissolve negativity in any chakra and, of course, as its name implies, it is very useful when working with any disorders of the blood. It is also good for nervous disorders and insomnia.

Suggested placings   The feet to the pelvis. The spine. Along any broken or fractured bones. On any chakra where negativity is encountered. On the forehead to draw out heat from a fever. On damaged joints.

RUBY CRYSTAL - deep wine red opaque, six-sided crystal.

A ruby crystal is very special, particularly if it contains an equilateral triangle. This is a 'record keeper' and links it to the Akashic Records, which is the Memory Bank of "All that is". It can be very helpful in healing, as it helps the body remember and release "Old Stuff" that may be held in the physical, or other energetic bodies surrounding the physical body. It is a stone to carry or wear, for protection against psychic attack. If you suffer unpleasant dreams, place one under your pillow. In the physical, it detoxifies the body and blood. It also treats fevers and restricted blood flow.

Suggested placings   The feet to the pelvis   The heart. Above the head, at a distance of 5 inches or 12.5 centimetres. When led to use it, place it in position before you commence the healing.

NOTE: You could also use Rhodocrosite, Copper or Carnelian on this chakra.

STONES FOR THE SACRAL CHAKRA

CARNELIAN – burnt orange to orange in colour.

This crystal is very much a crystal of the emotions. It helps to banish sorrow, fear, envy and anger. It also can be used to dispel apathy, indolence and passivity. Even further, it can help to increase personal power, creativity and compassion. On the physical level, it can be used to increase energy, also to treat neuralgia, gall stones, kidney stones, pollen allergies and colds. It can help in disorders of the spine, spleen and pancreas. It can be used to heal cuts and abrasions. I remember being on the Greek Island of Patmos several years ago and buying, instinctively, a small piece of Carnelian to place on a very persistent leg ulcer, which then soon disappeared.

Suggested placings This crystal, while being specially recommended for use on the sacral chakra area, can beneficially be used on the heart, solar plexus and root chakras also.

COPPER – bright copper colour, irregular in shape.

Copper is good for activating and opening both the Root and sacral chakras. It helps the evolution of one's intuition. It is said to be linked with the planet Venus and therefore with the energies of vitality, sexuality and desire. It carries very much a female energy quality. It can help to combat lethargy, passivity and restlessness, as well as excitability and non – acceptance of oneself, and one's destiny. It can conduct electrical impulses and can magnify the energy transfer from either the healer or the other crystals being used, to the healee. Copper can help stabilise and balance the flow of blood within the body and increase circulatory functions when necessary. It can be used in the treatment of arthritis and rheumatism, and to stimulate metabolic rate.

Suggested placings   Root chakra, Sacral chakra, or Solar Plexus chakra.

GOLDEN TIGER EYE – warm honey brown tones.

Historically, because of its glow, Tiger eye was believed to improve eyesight, prevent eye diseases and avert the 'Evil Eye'. It is good for grounding, aids concentration and focuses energy to meet challenges. Being linked to the energy of the tiger, it is symbolic of inner strength. It encourages optimism, enhances creativity, which is always beneficial in the healing process, and balances both the yin-yang energy, and the left and right hemispheres of the brain. It is an emotionally stabilising crystal. In addition, it can help mend broken bones, aid the reproductive system and clear bowel constrictions.

Suggested placings. Root and Sacral chakras. It can also be useful for gentle attunement of the Third Eye.

GOLDEN TOPAZ – the colour of barley sugar.

Topaz recharges. It has characteristics of a battery and is a crystal which works particularly well alongside silver, as silver amplifies its potential. Silver itself is an excellent conductor of energy. It is also worth noting that topaz combines well with amethyst for healing, producing a soothing, clearing and stabilising effect. Topaz helps raise energy levels and cleans the aura. It is a crystal with soothing qualities, helping one to remotivate and creatively change one's personal world. It helps one tap into inner resources, promoting truth, understanding and forgiveness in a situation. It can be used in the treatment of problems of the liver, gall bladder and endocrine glands. It has also proved useful in restoring the sense of taste, clearing skin eruptions and in the healing of wounds.

<u>Suggested placings</u> Root, Sacral and Solar Plexus chakras, also the Crown chakra. It has a 'Regal' quality, and is sometimes known as Imperial Topaz.

STONES FOR THE SOLAR PLEXUS CHAKRA

CITRINE– pale yellow to orange

Much of the 'citrine' sold is actually artificially heat-treated amethyst, so you need to check with your supplier. This fact may not put you off, rather you need to be aware of what you are buying. Much of the genuine citrine comes from the Ural Mountains in Russia. It encourages openness and optimism and dispels fear. It is excellent for energising and cleansing and is, in fact the only crystal I know which is said to never need cleansing. It promotes mental clarity and emotional maturity, while clearing negativity. It penetrates problems and expedites solutions, especially within a family or group. Especially in its faceted form, it stimulates the crown chakra. It is known as a 'Merchant's Stone' and is said to be good for the acquisition and retention of wealth. It is useful for its ability to balance the yin/yang energies and for aligning the chakras of the physical body with the ethereal plane. More specifically it is useful in treating digestive disorders and in promoting good circulation of the blood. It can be used in the treatment of degenerative disorders, and to shrink growths. Also it aids clarity of vision, balances the thyroid and activates the thymus, which both stimulates the immune system and strengthens ties with the Angelic Realm.

<u>Suggested placings</u>   Solar plexus, thymus, crown

AMBER – orange/yellow semi-transparent.

Amber is a fossilised resin. It aids healing by transmuting energy in the body from negative to positive. It is a sacred stone to both Eastern Indians and North American Indians. It purifies body, mind and spirit, and helps any broken elements of these three. As our arms and hands are the 'tools' we use in our work, amber is excellent for any problems, both emotional and physical, in these areas.

It may be used in the treatment of goitre and other diseases of the throat. It may also be used in treating problems of the kidneys and bladder. It is excellent anywhere where gentle energy is called for.

Suggested placings   Sacral, Solar plexus, throat

SUNSTONE – burnt orange opaque.

Sunstone is an obvious choice for the solar plexus chakra, because of its link to the energy of the sun, but it may not be easy for you to find. Its character is bright, cleansing and invigorating. It seems to be full of sparkle because of the tiny inclusions which constantly reflect the available light. These may be either hematite or goethite, and therefore their properties should also be considered. It is useful for cleansing and brightening the aura, releasing a build-up of invading psychic energy. It helps alleviate stress and fearfulness, aiding one in becoming one's own person. The solar plexus is the energy centre of both the soul and the ego and as such is fundamental in helping the break through to the spiritual nature of the individual. Basically speaking, the more the soul grows the less egotistical connections matter, and of course it works the other way around as well, in that the more one is caught up in issues of the ego the less energy is available for spiritual growth. Ancient cultures revered the sunstone as being sacred and central to their worship of the sun. On the physical level it is used to relieve stomach tensions and heal ulcers. It has been used to help sore throats and to assist in the healing of cartilage problems. It may be found helpful in dealing with rheumatism, as it helps one to 'lighten up' and be less rigid in both mind and body.

Suggested placings.   Solar Plexus, around the throat, and on the site of cartilage damage

GOLD (sometimes sold as gold leaf, suspended in fluid, as illustrated.)

Gold is a difficult recommendation for me to make because of the prohibitive cost. Nine carat gold is not really suitable because that means there are only nine parts of gold in twenty-four, in other words it contains fifteen parts of something else, quite often largely nickel. This is the usual quality of gold sold in the UK. while European gold is often fourteen carat. If, however, you are fortunate enough to know a 'craft' jeweller, they may be prepared to sell you a small piece of eighteen carat gold, (eighteen parts to twenty-four), or if you are lucky enough to own a gold coin the percentage will be very close to one hundred per cent. Gold is known as the Master Healer. It is an excellent purifier of the physical body. When you think that the site of pain is usually the site of a build-up of toxins, you will understand how important this is. Gold stands for the Light aspect of the Divine, and can put us in touch with qualities of the same. Its bright shininess helps us overcome aspects of depression and inferiority and increase vitality. As well as its link to the Solar plexus it is also linked to the development, balancing and purification of the heart chakra. Its energy is linked to that of the sun and it is held sacred for many ancient cultures. It, in its pure form is completely non corrosive, and has been taken excavated out of the earth during archaeological digs looking as fresh and untouched as it looked thousands of years before. Therefore it holds the qualities of constancy and endurance. Gold may be used to open and activate the third eye and crown chakras. When other crystals are placed near gold, it helps to maintain the qualities of those crystals, for example, in a jewellery setting, or to 'hold on' the energy of a particular crystal in a Healing crystal placement. On a physical level, gold is excellent for use with arthritis and rheumatism sufferers, for helping to rebuild the nervous system, for example with people who suffer from multiple sclerosis, in the treatment of shingles, or after a replacement operation of a body part, for example a hip replacement. Gold may be placed on the site of cancer and may also be applied anywhere where there is pain or discomfort, and well as for balancing the left and right brain, for example in autism.

Suggested placings   Solar plexus, heart, third eye and crown.

PINK STONES FOR THE HEART CHAKRA

ROSE QUARTZ - Very pale to pale pink.

Rose Quartz is an all-time favourite among healing crystals. It has a wonderful soft and gentle energy which is very soothing and calming in any situation. People who are traumatised in any way are helped by the energies which rose quartz filters through. Think of the different crystals as keyholes, allowing rites of passage to certain energies. This filtering process, because of the awareness, or gnosis, (wisdom with knowledge) we show in the choosing, allows certain beneficent energies from the Spirit Realm to make themselves available to us. In fact this is one of the crystals that I have in quite a large size, the size of a reasonable piece of coal, in my collection. This is known as a Master Crystal, which is to do with its size or perceived power, or both. On occasion, this has gone out to those in great distress, for example on the death of a loved one, when someone we love is dangerously ill, or when a beloved partner walks out, to specially focus the energy of Divine Love towards the grieving person for a while. However, don't lend something if you cannot afford to lose it. It would be better to either suggest the person buy one for themselves or that you give them a small piece. Each one of these forays, however, makes the crystal itself stronger and capable of transmuting more and more energy. It would be good to refresh the crystal on its return, under running water for a minute or two and to blow on it three times to re-attune it to your own special energy. It is lovely to be able to give someone in pain a small crystal to help them, and, if in doubt as to which one, rose quartz is always a good choice. You might even like to keep a small collection for the purpose. The basic message of Rose Quartz is LOVE, including all-important self love, and helps one to be oneself loving. It can be used to attune each chakra to the proper energy frequency and to aid both physical and emotional rejuvenation.

Suggested placings   As before mentioned, it can be used on any chakra, and is particularly useful when working on the root chakra with anyone with a heart problem, where a red crystal would be too strong. It is also particularly useful of course, on the heart, concerning feminine heart problems. This does not mean that you would never use it when working with a man. It is perfect, for example, when the man has problems associated with love around the females in his life. It is also very useful when dealing with love emotions and related physical emanations form these problems, in any chakra above the heart, that is to say, the thymus, throat, third eye and crown.

RHODOCROSITE – in the rosy pink colour range.

These crystals are very beautiful in my opinion. Again, this crystal is about love and balance, but in an even more refined and subtle way than Rose Quartz. It has, some would say, an Angelic, other worldly power beautifully linking it to Love. It is infiltrated and surrounded by a golden energy and if you decide to get one, don't be in a hurry to get a special piece, but wait to find one which you feel has the magical qualities that I have tried to express here. It is a crystal for balancing the Root, Sacral, Heart and Thymus chakras in particular, but it is compassionate in nature and is therefore soothing to any area of the body which has been negatively affected physically, by strain resulting from the person's overworked compassionate behaviour. It is an excellent stone for use in meditation. It is very useful in getting rid of the unwanted stuff in terms of emotion and also in elimination on the physical level and therefore, for example can be used in problems with the intestines and those of the proper production of fluids necessary to the digestive system. It can be used to regulate the heart and pulse rates and also in thyroid imbalances.

Suggested placings   Root, Sacral, Heart and Thymus chakras

PINK TOURMALINE - Sugar pink opaque.

Tourmaline is a crystal much revered by shamen of African, Native American and Aboriginal tribes, for its healing powers and powers of protection. It is a stone of insight, therefore banishing fear and pain. It has been called the stone of 'Knowing'. It is also a stone for balancing the left and right sides of the brain. In its pink form it is a crystal particularly linked to creativity and confidence to try the 'new'. It promotes joy and a sense of peace during periods of change and growth. Once more, of course, it is a crystal linked to the Love and Understanding energies. As we are working up the body you will notice that the crystal characteristics are becoming more subtle and in a way less specific, their specific use being more reliant on the attunement of the practitioner. If this makes you feel concern then simply return for a while to the crystal tabulation provided, but also remember that whatever the question, Love is the answer : that if your intent is impeccable and you are working with an open heart and mind, your intuition, the link with your guides, is bound to grow. When definite messages are dropped into your mind, as they will eventually be, have the courage to act on them, and then stand back and assess the results!

This is a crystal said to protect one from falls, and will also assuage problems resulting from falls. This works on both a physical and metaphysical level. It has energies of holism: in other words, it unites the disparate parts of the body, in order that it comes together as a whole, so that a disease be helped in a consolidated manner. It has been used to treat disorders of the heart, lungs and skin.

<u>Suggested placings</u> Heart and Thymus and Crown chakras, but also anywhere that needs to be integrated with the rest of the body, and anywhere where there is a problem with the skin. Also for balance, on the left and right sides of the brain.

GREEN STONES FOR THE HEART CHAKRA

MALACHITE- Dark green shading to pale green.

Malachite is particularly a stone of transformation, and so it is interesting that years ago when I knew nothing of such things I bought a little green malachite frog, an excellent representation for transformation from young tadpole to adult frog. It helps us to receive insights that enable us to 'grow up'. It is excellent for supporting any male heart energy problem, with a man or with a woman who needs help either in developing her male side or in dealing with the male(s) in her life. Malachite is green because it has a high concentration of copper and so it is good for relieving inflammation and swelling as well as relaxing tension. It helps with deep feelings of hurt and resentment and also helps cut unwanted ties. On the physical level it is good for treating asthma, arthritis, swollen joints growths and tumours. It aligns DNA and cellular structure and enhances the immune system. It is also said to aid creativity and to relieve the process of birth, either on the physical or emotional planes, as in rebirthing.

<u>Suggested placings</u> Heart, Thymus and Throat chakras, also any pain areas of the body

DARK GREEN JADE - usually dark bottle green and almost opaque.

Jade is a stone of protection against negative forces. You will see in the tabulation that I have listed both dark green jade and pale jade. The dark one is deep bottle green, slightly mottled and opaque in colour. It has a waxy feel. The pale jade is **very delicate in colour**. It varies from very pale green/white opaque to pale blue/green opaque. In a way I hesitate to recommend jade because it may take you time to find what you are looking for, but it is well worth the search. It is confusing because jade is often called Jadeite, Transvaal Jade or Nephrite and may look more like onyx and be slightly translucent, like a green grape. Personally, instinctively I have never felt drawn to this form, jadeite being the one I'm drawn to, but you may find Nephrite easier to obtain and possibly cheaper. It is also possible to fake jade as it is many other things. This just illustrates once again the necessity of always buying your precious crystals from someone you feel you can trust. The paler jade which I possess is more delicate and subtle and therefore can be used where a more delicate quality of healing is called for, or with the higher chakras, thymus, throat and even third eye. Jade has long been revered by "primitive " tribes as a sacred stone. It is a stone of very gentle energy and is said to promote a very gentle transition from this world to the next. This can be the Dream World, a state of altered consciousness or even death. It is strongly connected to the realm of dreams and their realisation. It helps to attune oneself to the needs of ourselves and others and helps us access the wisdom necessary to support the expedition of those needs. It can be used in the treatment of the heart, hips, kidneys and spleen. Jadeite is a stone of status and could only be possessed by the elite of the realm. It was often used for carving figures of the gods and goddesses. It can be used to reunite or bind together. This could apply to cellular or skeletal damage. The emerald green variety of jadeite, known as imperial jade, may be used to improve dysfunctional relationships or to aid cohesiveness and co-operation in a group

Suggested placings The heart.

GREEN TOURMALINE (bottle green opaque)

This crystal is a stone of the heart and of compassion, but with a 'masculine' strength and determination about it. It is useful in rectifying problems one may be experiencing with the male figures in one's life. Also it is strongly connected to the green plant kingdom and can be used to help one in both the study and practice of herbalism and flower essences. It helps attunement between matters of the heart, (love and compassion) and matters of the third eye, (visions, insights and understandings). In a healing context, it could be placed first on the heart and then on the third eye help to establish the development of insights. It is said to attract success, prosperity and abundance. It is used in situations of regeneration of the heart, the thymus and the immune system.

Suggested placings. The heart, Thymus or Third Eye.

APPLE GREEN CHRYSOPRASE - may range from a pale blue-green through to fairly dark grass green, opaque.

Chrysoprase is a wonderful crystal for calming the emotions and lowering the blood pressure. It is a excellent aid to restful relaxed sleep. It is actually an apple green type of chalcedony, and, as such is useful for balancing the energies of the body, mind, emotions, and spirit. It activates, opens and energises the Heart Chakra, and is a particular favourite of mine. It stimulates non-judgemental attitudes, as well as acceptance of oneself and others. It can also bring about healing to a 'broken heart' situation and promote understanding as to such difficult patterns of growth. It can be used in treatment of disorders of the heart, in situations of infirmity and frailty, to increase the assimilation of vitamin C and to help increase fertility.

<u>Suggested placings</u> The Heart and Crown Chakras.

KUNZITE A form of spodumene. Very pale mauve-pink, glasslike.

This mineral activates the heart chakra and third eye. It aids loving thoughts and loving communication. It radiates a powerful sense of peace. It connects us with the infinite source of love. It helps us to express emotions of the heart in a confident and relaxed way. It is a facilitator which helps us attain that which we need for our physical, emotional and intellectual development. It dissolves negativity and can be used to remove obstacles from one's path as long as the removal acts in the truly best interests of those concerned. It enables one to remain calm in the midst of distraction. A piece held vertically will align and balance all chakras and bestow an energy of peace and centredness. Although encouraging a maturity of thought it can help one to retain the open-mindedness of a child. On a physical level it can help strengthen the muscles of the heart, and can also prove useful in treating disorders of the lungs and circulatory systems. It has a been used to clear blockages in the physical body and stimulate and regulate good hormonal function. It is an excellent crystal for working with young energy.

<u>Suggested placings</u> Heart and Third Eye chakras.

STONES FOR THE THYMUS

TURQUOISE - Colour ranges from fairly pale to deep intense colour. If you can't decide, buy two, for use on different occasions. Then, when you need to use turquoise get the pendulum to choose which one you should use.

Turquoise is a supreme stone of attunement: attunement between the physical and spiritual worlds, also attunement between individuals who each possess psychically attuned stones, the stones being introduced to each other, with the intention of recognition and attunement. It is also known in many cultures as a stone of strength, and protection against negative energies of all kinds. It stimulates the thymus gland which is involved with the immune system, so it helps to protect against disease also. Although it is linked with the energy of 'Father Sky' it is an excellent stone for grounding. It carries a very soothing energy, bringing peace of mind. It can be used to balance the male and female aspects of one's character. It enhances one's abilities for trust, kindness and the recognition of beauty. It is a master healer.

Suggested placings   Turquoise may be placed on the thymus and anywhere on the body, as it has the ability to balance and align all chakras. Just follow your intuition for when and how to use it, including carrying or wearing it, or placing it in your environment.

CHRYSOCOLLA - deep blue-green colour, usually with grey or black inclusions.

Chrysocolla is known as a woman's best friend! (or those working with their feminine side.) It is a revitalising and calming crystal. It can generate great inner strength both through the ability to act or refrain from action. It can sustain one when peacemaking is called for. In truth, it helps one to develop the 'goddess' state of womanhood. It is concerned with realignment of the Self, that is to say it helps us to attune to the perfection of the universe, and helps us intuit that information which is necessary for the physical body, the intellect and the emotions in order to help us re-align to that which we truly are. Further, it can help those working in the field of Earth energies to understand what is needed in order that the Earth heal herself. It can help the regeneration of the pancreas, the regulation of insulin and the balancing of blood sugar. It strengthens the muscular structure of the legs arms and back and has been used in working with various disorders of the blood, including leukaemia. In addition it is a useful crystal in working with disorders of the lungs, tuberculosis, asthma and emphysema for example.

Suggested placings   Root, Sacral and Solar plexus chakras as well as Heart and Throat chakras.

ANGELITE - pale blue, often opaque.

This crystal is a gift to the earth from the angelic realms. It is the stone of astrologers and mathematicians It symbolises the communication of love and light to the world. A favourite greeting of my friends and I to each other is "Love and Light." It is excellent for balancing and aligning the physical body and for placing a protective shield around it. It acts as an interconnecting mechanism between this and other worlds, granting communication with one's angels and animal totems, aiding both astral travel and journeys of the spirit while possibly opening up the opportunities for channelling. It represents peace and dispels anger, which sometimes translates as inflammation in the physical body. It can help correct problems with the heart, throat and thymus. It is linked to Lifeblood and helps renew blood vessels while correcting deficiencies of the haemoglobin.

Suggested placings Sites of inflammation. Heart, Throat and Thymus.

PALE JADE - Pale green to almost white in colour.

This is a particular favourite of mine. I have a pale green jade Kwan Yin, illustrated, and a pale green miniature Buddha in my collection. Working at the level of the thymus is working with the immune system, and also working at a very subtle level spiritually. We could say working with the Angelic forces. Pale jade, in my experience, has a very subtle energy to it, just right for working with these energies. In particular, in addition to the qualities mentioned under Jade, are two properties of jade which work at this level of subtlety. One is, and I quote from 'Love is in the Earth', which touches me very deeply: "As the visible world is nourished by the invisible, humanity can be sustained and preserved by the lovely visions of dreamers. One who reveres a beautiful vision or ideal can utilise the energies of jade to assist in realising those thoughts. Jade helps one to cherish ones desires and facilitates the building of one's dreams in this physical reality. It releases ones limitations such that permission is granted which allows one to actualise aspirations and to attain limitless achievements. It inspires and induces ambition toward the accomplishment of objectives."

And secondly it can act as a stitching agent, mending both things which have been cut or torn, in cellular or skeletal physical form, or helping psychological damage and hurt to be healed by pale jade's gentle and loving energy.

<u>Suggested placings</u>   Thymus, Throat (linked to self expression both verbally and creatively) and Third eye.

STONES FOR THE THROAT CHAKRA

BLUE LACE AGATE Called in Russia, where it comes from, the landscape stone. It is pale blue in colour.

This crystal helps one enter into higher frequency states of awareness, when used in regions of the Heart, Third Eye and Crown, as well as the throat chakras. It is a gentle stone for gentle people. Psychically, it helps strengthen the skeletal structure and helps mend breaks and fractures. It helps remove blockages from the fine ends of the nervous system and from the capillaries of the circulatory system. It helps treat those glands associated with the digestive system, particularly the pancreas. It can also help treat outwardly manifested growths. It can help to regulate fluid around the brain, for example in cases of hydrocephalus. It is also said to soothe the eyes.

<u>Suggested placings</u> Throat, Heart, Third Eye and Crown.

AQUAMARINE - Colour range from light blue to green. As with many crystals, gem quality will be clearer, but you will more usually find opaque specimens, which are suitable for healing purposes. The clearer the crystal the more refined and subtle the energy.

This is a stone linked to the intellect and learning, not only about the physical world we live in, but about oneself. Also it works on alignment of the chakras, and helps connect the physical and ethereal bodies in order to provide an energy of wholeness in a person In addition it helps us bring about a balanced attitude to our lives, emotionally, intellectually and spiritually. It works well at the level of the throat chakra, in order to promote communication with others. Further, it helps us understand and work towards an attitude of service to others in this world, particularly in connection with healing. Physically it helps swollen glands and can also be used to strengthen glands. In addition it is also excellent in working with eyes, and formative bone structure of all kinds, including teeth. I have a lovely gentle guide linked to me through aquamarine, which is excellent in helping children or the child in one.

Suggested placings. Throat and Crown chakras.

BLUE CELESTITE - Crystallises into a beautiful clear pale blue colour.

This is a crystal of Balance. It helps in balancing and stabilising the yin-yang energies within one, while perfecting in interactional balance of the chakras. It aids one in fluent communication which is interesting to the listener. It can, in certain right circumstances, provide access to and communication from the angelic realms. It assists clairaudience, that is to say being able to 'hear' messages from the world of spirit. Think of it as a crystal with stories to tell. Of course the balance within the person and their energy field, first spoken of here, would help the situation be right for such transference of knowledge. In addition it is said to be a stone for astral travel and for excellent dream recall. It is a stone for calmness and harmony and the dismissal of worries. This is an excellent crystal for those studying music, which is the only truly abstract art, and helps set the energy sight where any art, craft or skill of a delicate nature is coming from the realm of spirit perfection into form, for example watercolour, jewellery or fine surgery. It is an excellent Healing stone, cleaning the energy in the area affected, transmuting pain and chaos into light and love. It may be used in the treatment of disorders of the eyes, to increase the range of hearing, and to balance mental disfunction. It can be used in the treatment of digestive disorders and in treating a dysfunctional intestinal system.

Suggested placings Throat, Sacral and Crown chakras in particular, eyes, ears and any place on the body where surgery has recently occurred.

BLUE SAPPHIRE - May be gem quality, as shown, or pale blue opaque, looking rather like aquamarine crystal illustration.

This may sound like a very expensive recommendation, but of course you do not need to buy a jem quality crystal. Sapphires occur in a wide variety of colours, but I am going to talk here only of the blue sapphire. The colour ties it particularly to the throat of course. I would also like to mention in passing the existence of a Madagascan Sapphire crystal, which has recently been available.

These are superior crystals, exhibiting extra qualities, including connection to metaphysical realms and, in certain circumstances, access to ancient scripts covering information about the past lives and physical movements of people coming to me for help. The circumstances of which I speak are during Past Life regression therapy, which I have been carrying out very successfully with the help of a colleague for some eight years now. Of course that is another huge subject and deserving of another book of its own some time.

The sapphire, in general, is a crystal for getting rid of unwanted thoughts and bringing one to a state of peace and happiness. It is a crystal which radiates its energy without conscious initiation, making it a good choice for a piece of jewellery, and so it is a traditional choice for an engagement ring. It is said to be the crystal surface on which Moses wrote the ten commandments and to have been one of the stones used in the breastplate of the High Priest, who was originally Moses' brother Aaron. The sapphire has been used in the treatment of disorders of the blood, in combating excessive bleeding and to strengthen the walls of veins. It has also been used to treat cellular disorders and to bring about their further 'co-operation'.

The blue sapphire can be used on all parts of the body for healing, but is particularly suited to working with the throat chakra, especially in assisting with communication. Once again there is an element of mystical knowledge and information from the akashic records associated with this crystal, possibly stemming from its link to the Ten Commandments. In addition, it can also assist in purifying and rectifying disjointed trapped energy which is inhibiting growth in the physical or mental development of one's life.

<u>Suggested placings</u> This is a stone of intuition and learning, and although its colour would link it particularly to the Throat and Third Eye chakras, it could be usefully be placed wherever you felt guided to do so. It is good for healing wounds.

STONES FOR THE THIRD EYE CHAKRA

SODALITE - colour, dark blue. (It does appear in other colours also.)
This is a stone particularly for the head. It helps one to think and to know, both working through logical processes and simply knowing. It works on left hand intellectual brain and right intuitive brain. It accommodates unemotional deduction, practical responses and lightness of heart. It is an excellent stone for use in groups, bringing about a group dynamic and an attitude of common purpose within the group. It fosters companionship and interdependency, encouraging self trust and trust in others. It further helps one to discern and understand true feelings and even, under certain circumstances, to access the sacred laws of the universe, as it has been used to open and clear the vision in the third eye. It works with problems of pains in the head, such as migraines and

FIRST
CHOICE

Red Jasper

Carnelian

Amber

Rose quartz

Malachite

Turquoise

Blue lace agate

Sodalite

Amethyst

SECOND
CHOICE

Garnet

Copper

Citrine

Rhodocrosite

Dark Green Jade

Chrysocolla

Aquamarine

lapis lazuli

Opal

THIRD CHOICE

Hematite

Golden tiger eye

Sunstone

Pink tourmaline

Green tourmaline

Angeltite

Blue Celestite

Moonstone

Herkimer diamond

FOURTH CHOICE

Ruby crystal

Golden topaz

Gold

Kunzite

Chrysoprase

Pale jade

Blue sapphire

Motther of pearl

Charoite

headaches, as well as giddiness and an inability to balance

Suggested placings Third Eye, right and left hemispheres of the brain, the back of the head, down as far as the base of the neck

LAPIS LAZULI - deep blue, sometimes containing pyrite, with the appearance of flecks of gold.

This crystal is very special, and is said to grant access to the sacred texts and mysteries, but in a way, at certain times and under certain conditions, in my experience all crystals have this attribute. Of course we then require the wisdom and understanding to unravel the information. Afghanistan is very famous for its lapis and the lapis found there is often flecked with pyrite, looking like a night sky bedecked with stars, connecting between the physical plane and the celestial kingdom. Lapis helps to awaken and expand awareness of the self, helping us on our long journey of evolution upward to the unification with "all that is". It is said to be a stone of courage. It is revered as a sacred and protective stone by the Tibetans, along with turquoise and amber. King Solomon was said to have possessed a Lapis ring which gave him great power over the dark forces. Certainly it helps one overcome depression and leads one to a state of at least relative serenity. It also can protect against psychic attacks.

Lapis is a stone for the third eye and may also be used successfully when working on the thymus, bone marrow, immune system, prevention and rectification of damage to the RNA/DNA system. It can also be used to access energy for oneself from the universal energy field. It may be used in disorders of the throat, especially when these disorders are linked to frustrations around creativity in some form.

Suggested placings Third eye, Thymus and Throat chakras.

MOONSTONE - usually displays a milky sheen somewhere on its surface, and sometimes a beautiful reflective pale blue colour.

The moon is connected to the soft, feminine, Yin energy of Woman. There is a contemporary Irish poet called John O'Donaghue, who wrote in his poem, 'The Nativity', " No man reaches where the moon touches a woman." There is something very beautiful and true about that line, and fundamental also. It is a stone for feeling, and understanding, via intuition and emotional thoughts. It is not to do with simply Man and Woman but to do with the quality of male and female energy melded together within us all. It is also to do with perception, discernment and mystery, the reflection in a celestial mirror. It gently cleanses negativity from the chakras, enhancing positive attributes of loving compassion and self expression. It also guides one in the way of the most practical route to attain that which one seeks. It is sustaining, gentle and calm and can imbue one with the quality of patience and a sense of "Right timing". It stimulates regeneration within the body. It helps the body to absorb good things (nutrients) and release bad things (toxins), so it helps the digestion and elimination systems. As the moon controls the tides on this planet, so moonstone can help to control the flow of water in our bodies. It can also aid circulatory disorders or where we have bodily swellings, for example bee stings or mosquito bites. Because of its particular link to the Divine Feminine, it is also helpful in promoting ease in pregnancy and childbirth, to enhance fertility and alleviate problems with pre menstrual tension and menopause.

Suggested placings   Third Eye and Sacral chakras.

PEARL

I was given a most beautiful grey pearl by a dear friend of mine who herself was given it by a pearl fisherman. He had just brought it up from the depths of the ocean!   It stands, of course, primarily for wisdom, and helps provide a clear channel for the advancement of this state, through the receipt of spiritual guidance. It represents also purity, innocence, faith and love.

It helps to calm one down and to bring about a contemplative state, enabling one to see a situation for what it is. It may be used to treat the soft organs of the body, because of its ability to exist with the soft tissue of the oyster, and to both increase fertility and ease childbirth.

Suggested placings   Thymus and Third Eye

MOTHER OF PEARL/Abalone Shell – pearly, often reflecting back many magical colours.

This has been revered by ancient tribes all over the world as a magical gift from the sea. It is an embodiment of the Archetypal Mother energy. It instils a stable, loving atmosphere whenever and wherever it is used and can stimulate fertility both of the mind and the body.

It also can be used for protection, particularly from uncooperative attitudes and actions. It can be used to treat hearing disorders, in the healing of breaks in the skeletal structure and to help the assimilation of vitamins. It can also protect the muscular system and prevent atrophy.

Suggested placings   Sacral and Third Eye chakras.

STONES FOR THE CROWN CHAKRA

AMETHYST Pale lavender to deep purple in colour.

This is a stone of transmutation, changing the vibrations of lower energies into those of higher energies. It provides a clear contact between the Earth plane and other worlds. It is good for clearing the aura and stabilising energy situations. It invigorates and yet instils peace. Amethyst is a good stone for protection against psychic attacks. It helps one to live up to one's responsibilities, and act from a "common sense" point of view. It helps us assimilate new ideas, and move on if we are feeling "stuck". It is a crystal which has long been used to help people with problems of alcohol, or substance abuse. In Roman times people used goblets made of amethyst, in order not to feel the need to fill them up again! Holding amethyst is said to help a speaker during debate. Together with Chlorite it is said to facilitate the removal of negative energy implants from within the body, because these crystals, in combination, provide a connection with Universal Mind. In the physical body amethyst is good for helping people with hearing problems, to strengthen the skeleton and help posture problems. It helps the nervous system and problems with the endocrine glands. It can also be useful in treating cellular disorders, where the condition is causing distress, helping the cells to readjust and realign. Amethyst is good with problems concerning insomnia and also headaches, in fact it can be placed on any area of the body to soak up pain.

<u>Suggested placings</u>   Throat and Crown chakras

OPAL   It is good to use this still attached to its host rock. It can however have a smooth and shiny surface.

Opal comes in many colour ranges and names. My specimens shine with a multiplicity of colours and are still attached to the Mother rock. In my collection I actually have three, one from Australia, one from America and one from Russia. This is because I find that one of these will be more suited to my client than the other two. (I have also got several turquoise, red jasper, rose quartz and amethyst for the same reason.)   Opals show a multiplicity of spectral colours because, under a microscope, you would see that they are built up from discs stacked one on the other, each refracting a different wavelength of light. Opals do in fact amplify one's characteristics, making them easier to pick up on and therefore deal with. They enhance feelings also, allowing us the means for expression and release. They are good for helping the memory and also good for loyalty and faithfulness, in both personal and business affairs. It is said, in certain circumstances, they are able to help one become invisible, to fade into the background when one does not wish to be seen. Conversely opal allows one's aspirations to surface, in order to aid progress. Opal is a crystal for helping awaken the higher powers of intuition and mysticism. When an opal exhibits flashes of bright colour in it it is particularly suited to this purpose. The flashes of bright colour represent one's inner flame. It has been used in the Australian, Aboriginal and American Indian traditions to invoke visions and vision quests, the Shaman astral travelling, in order to retrieve parts of a person's soul which have been "stolen". Opal is used in the physical body to disperse infections and purify the blood. It can also be used to help heal disorders of the vision and eyes. It may be used to help those suffering from Parkinson's Disease and to help aid comfort and ease during childbirth.

<u>Suggested placings.</u> Third Eye and Crown chakras and abdomen.

HERKIMER DIAMOND   Clear double terminated stout prismatic pseudo-diamond crystal.

These were originally discovered in Herkimer, in the United States of America, in the oil fields there. Similar formations have since been found elsewhere. It is a crystal which allows us to "see ourselves clearly", and to begin again, should we not be happy with what we see, while realising that we do not have to "become" anything, that what we need is already there. Our job is to actualise our potential, and herkimer helps us to relax our unconscious fears and worries that are preventing us from doing so. It is a stone of attunement, not only to the self but to another person, environment or activity. Therefore herkimer can help in telepathic communication with another person or in situations of clairvoyance or clairaudience. As with all quartz, it can accept and retain information which can be retrieved at another time and place. It is a good crystal to use to release tensions and anxieties in both the physical body and the energetic bodies which surround the physical body. It also helps in the recovery of memory in various parts of the body, allowing those parts to remember how they were and therefore facilitate healing. Herkimer is also useful for helping toxins which have accumulated in the body to disperse and to correct imbalances in both the metabolic rate and the RNA/DNA structures.

Suggested placings   Where release of tension or remembering is necessary, Third Eye and Crown.

CHAROITE - pale mauve, may be mottled with purple, pink or grey/black.

This crystal is particularly found in Russia, and is highly revered there for having Healing qualities and when I was in Russia a few years ago I was lucky enough to procure a special piece. It is a stone for this age as it provides for a strong link between the Crown and the Heart chakras, that is to say between the higher spiritual dimensions and a conscious shift towards unconditional love on the physical plane. Charoite helps us to be able to let go of past hurts. It helps us to accept "all kinds and conditions of men", in order that we allow a base line from which to go forward together, in an energy situation of help, support and love, albeit sometimes tough love, but trying to maintain a situation of what is truly best for all. It helps us in analytical abilities and precision, providing for careful sifting through while investigating the unknown. In addition it helps us both to realise and accept that we are just where we need to be at any time, not for what we want, but for what we need. It also helps us to accept and love ourselves, "warts and all", as we are surely loved understood and accepted by the Creator or Higher Power. This is a base line situation and it does not mean that things will not be put in our path and that hurdles will not be placed there also, which we may be encouraged to jump, for this is the way in which we learn and grow. We do not find it easy to grow when things are easy, comfortable and happy ; we need to be challenged. On a physical level charoite can be used to treat disorders of the eyes and heart, aid autism and help in degenerate conditions of the liver, due to excess alcohol and the pancreas, due to excess refined sugar consumption, which we need to be more vigilant about as it is added in such unnecessarily large amounts to so many processed foods these days. Charoite will also help stimulate and regulate the blood pressure and pulse.

<u>Suggested placings</u>   The Heart, Third Eye and Crown Chakras.

MASTER CRYSTALS

I have several, as I call them, Master Crystals. These have been acquired over the years as I have come upon them. What are they? Well, first of all they are large in size, but apart from that I feel they carry more energy. How do I use them? When someone is about to receive healing energy, I always ask if I should give them one of these Master Crystals to hold, and further, whether they should hold it in their right or left hand. I believe their purpose is to amplify the Healing power in some way. In the crystal ranges that we are discussing at the moment, I have Master Crystal versions of the following, which have been gathered up over many years:

Red jasper   Citrine   Rose quartz   Malachite   Turquoise   Amethyst   Rhodocrosite   Chrysocolla   Lapis lazuli   and   Quartz

Suggested crystals for use with the eight main chakras. We do not require large crystals in the main for healing purposes, as they are to be placed on or around the body.

Chakra	First Choice	Second Choice	Third Choice	Fourth Choice
Root	Red jasper	Garnet	Hematite	Ruby crystal
Sacral	Carnelian	Copper	Golden Eye Tiger	Golden topaz
Solar Plexus	Amber	Citrine	Sunstone	Gold
Heart	Rose quartz Malachite	Rhodocrosite Dark green jade	Pink tourmaline Green tourmaline	Kunzite Chrysoprase
Thymus	Turquoise	Chrysocolla	Angelite	Pale jade
Throat	Blue lace agate	Aquamarine	Blue Celestite	Blue sapphire
Third Eye	Sodalite	Lapis lazuli	Moonstone	Mother of pearl (Pearl is a further option)
Crown	Amethyst	Opal	Herkimer diamond	Charoite

I have listed these crystals somewhat on the basis of cost and availability, the ones in the first colomn being the easeist and cheapest to obtain. Choose stones that are fairly smooth and of a reasonable size as very small stones tend to get mislaid. I have however made an exception in the case of the blue sapphire in my collection. Each stone is compatible with all the others.

Chapter Ten

Part two of the pendulum language
Circles and ellipses

Please Note: There is generally no significance in the sizes of diagrams throughout this chapter.

As you already know, all four crosses of the pendulum language are shown enclosed within a circle, but, up to now, you have neither seen it or used it in your work. Now we are going to begin using the circle as part of the pendulum language. The rotation of the circle or ellipse on its own may be either clockwise of anticlockwise. If it is CLOCKWISE it has four possible interpretations –

THINKING/WORKING These two are linked together, similar to the Fear/Pain/Ignorance line.
LEARNING
ALWAYS or ETERNALLY

The most common translations for a clockwise circle, in my experience, is either THINKING or WORKING or the two in combination, THINKING/WORKING.

CLOCKWISE CIRCLE DIAGRAM

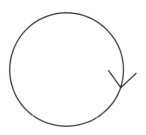

111

If the circle or ellipse rotates in an ANTICLOCKWISE DIRECTION, the possible translations are

ANXIETY   HURT   INSECURITY
DEPRESSION   FRUSTRATION
IRRITATION   APPREHENSION
ANGER   RESENTMENT

There is also the possibility of the interpretation being SOMETIMES because these two circles are in opposition to each other and ETERNALLY is balanced by SOMETIMES.

NEVER is obviously not an option in the world of the Spirit, because the pendulum simply refuses to move in response to the word NEVER!

ANTICLOCKWISE CIRCLE DIAGRAM

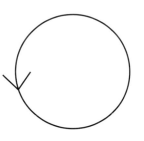

You may, at this point, feel concern for the seemingly large number of interpretations for two such simple movements, but I start, when interpreting, from the upright BALANCE LINE and try each interpretation in turn, while watching to see which word or combination of words takes the energy forward to the TRUTH LINE. Each correct interpretation you make will enable the pendulum to give you an axis, each additional axis taking the pendulum swing further over towards that all-important Truth Line. If you guess incorrectly the pendulum will give you an axis back towards the Balance Line again, rectifying the situation when you insert a correct guess. For example it could swing from BALANCE to YES on adding FRUSTRATION, and from YES to TRUTH on adding HURT to FRUSTRATION, or it could reach the TRUTH LINE from the BALANCE LINE with a combination of DEPRESSION, ANGER and HURT, moving closer to the TRUTH LINE with the addition of each correct word. (Notice the power of the word. How much more powerful might be the power of THE WORD, THE LOGOS. See the Near Death Experience, as recorded in Chapter One, which I unwittingly entitled "How it all began." !!)

Of course you then address your findings to the client to see their reactions and talk the situation through with them, helping them to recognise, clarify and resolve their feelings. Context makes for clarity in translation. The fact that you know how they feel, even when sometimes they have not been able to be clear on it for themselves, is of tremendous help to them, as it really helps them to understand. Insight and Understanding pushes out Fear and Pain, while Wisdom pushes out Ignorance, but the opposing words **can** work in any combination.

DIAGRAM SHOWING THE PROGRESSION FROM NEUTRAL BALANCE LINE TO THE TRUTH LINE THROUGH THREE PROGRESSIONS OF THE AXIS THROUGH DEPRESSION ANGER AND HURT.

Notice how Depression, Anger and Hurt occur in differing amounts

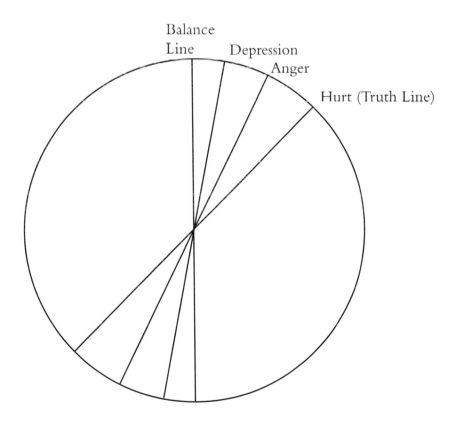

A very important point to remember is that a STRAIGHT LINE is known here as an AXIS, and you can have either clockwise or anticlockwise movement around an axis, which produces an ELLIPSE

DIAGRAM SHOWING
AN AXIS

DIAGRAM SHOWING AN
ELLIPSE AROUND AXIS

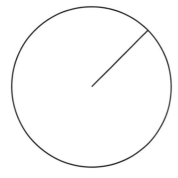

Thinking or working around the Spiritual or Unconditional Love would look as shown above, in the diagram showing the ELLIPSE. NOTE that the vertical axis would not be visible in the pendulum swing.

You would then ask the question of the pendulum, "Do you mean working?" No. "Do you mean thinking?" Truth. "Do you mean Around Unconditional Love?" No. "Do you mean around the spiritual?" Truth. Therefore the complete interpretation is that this person is thinking around the Spiritual, possibly their own connection with Spirituality. You can then use the pendulum on a Yes/ No basis to discover further shades of meaning. Is your "guess", of this being about themselves, correct? Do they think of the Divine in terms of God? Cosmic Mind? Earth Energies? You can see, I expect, what an advantage insights such as this would be in a counselling situation. You can speak with your client in their own terms.

Here is another example. A possible interpretation here could be, for example, taking the anticlockwise negative energy ellipse first, APPREHENSION. Around what? It could be GIFT. The choices are Love, Truth, Gift or Healing as that is what the axis stands for. It translates as – Apprehension around Gift. Maybe the person is just beginning to experience the paranormal for themselves. Maybe something dramatic, such as a bereavement, has caused the Third Eye chakra to open. They start seeing a loved one whom they believe, because they are "dead" cannot possibly be there. They could certainly suffer apprehension and wonder if they are going crazy. They certainly may not realise that this is, in fact, the beginning of a gift of clairvoyance. If you were their councillor, they might be very glad indeed that you had picked up on what was going on with them, and could offer them some reassurance and support.

Always try each possible translation in turn, (unless you are getting a clear signal in your mind) until one interpretation on its own, or a combination of interpretations, give you a sum total, working from the Balance Line, of that all important 45 degree angle to the Balance Line, the **Truth** Line.

NB The Love/Truth/Gift/Healing line axis below is PERCEIVED AND NOT SEEN.

DIAGRAM OF ELLIPSE
AROUND LOVE, TRUTH, GIFT,
HEALING LINE SHOWING
NEGATIVE EMOTION.
TRANSLATES AS
APPREHENSION AROUND
GIFT. SEE EXPLANATION
ABOVE

Note that the width of the ellipses can vary from very slim and narrow up to almost full circle and sometimes evolve into a circle, but more of this later. This would be due to the extent of negativity or positivity involved. The wider the ellipse the greater the energy involvement. As you can already see you can have a negative energy ellipse around a positive axis and a positive energy ellipse around a negatively positioned axis, e.g. the Fear /Pain line. (You can also have positive [clockwise] around positive and negative [anticlockwise] around negative. We will come to these later.)

Now let us look at clockwise movement forward from axis to axis.

Remember that when the pendulum is pushing forward (clockwise) in a series of straight axes, it means that the person is pushing forward from a difficult place, *or* attempting to move forward too fast. Remember the outer circle is drawn in merely to show DIRECTION or THRUST and is not in itself visible. NB Axes travelling in an ANTICLOCKWISE direction indicate BOXED IN, HEMMED IN, DO NOT KNOW WHICH WAY TO GO ENERGY.

DIAGRAM OF AXES PUSHING
FORWARDS/CLOCKWISE
WITHIN A CIRCLE

DIAGRAM OF AXES PUSHING
BACKWARDS/ANTICLOCKWISE
WITHIN A CIRCLE.

Sometimes we get ellipses, Daisy Loops, as I sometimes call them, as shown here, because there is even more energy, of a positive or negative character, present, causing the effect to occur.

DIAGRAM SHOWING FORWARD AXES HAVING BECOME ELLIPSES

There are no less than four different combinations possible now, because the energy of the outer circle, which represents the directional THRUST of the ellipses or so-called daisy loops as a whole, (but cannot itself be seen), can be travelling in both a clockwise or anticlockwise direction. The ellipses themselves can also have either a positive or negative thrust to them. In other words, it is possible for the general direction to be forward, clockwise (positive), while the energy of each ellipse is in fact backward, anticlockwise (negative).

POSITIVE AND POSITIVE DIAGRAM
Positive circle, Positive ellipses.

The thrust of the ellipses as a whole, is forward (positive).

The thrust of each individual ellipse, is also forward (positive).

This pattern of swing means "Pushing forward". This may be from a difficult place, and could also possibly mean "pushing forward too fast", but nevertheless, because of the added positive energy of ellipses instead of axes, WORKING, THINKING OR LEARNING, (or those energies in some combination) at the same time. If the pendulum does confirm that things are moving along too fast the person concerned may be well advised to slow down a little and take stock of the present situation a little more.

The degree of effort is shown by the NUMBER of the ellipses and the speed of progress is shown by the WIDTH of ellipses.(less ellipses -faster progress towards completion.) The more axes or more ellipses, over a given distance of the circumference of the outer enclosing circle (which remember is not in itself visible) the more difficult the task is proving and the longer the time needed to elapse for completion of the task. An example of the energy pattern shown above could be a person having lost their home. Obviously this is a difficult position to be in. (Maybe the loss had occurred because of the breakdown of a relationship, or the loss of their job.) However, they are handling the situation in a positive and thoughtful way, and, judging by the width of the loops, would find somewhere to live before too long. (Loops of the given width would not take long to reach the Truth/Healing line.)

SPECIAL PHENOMENON

Now take note of the special phenomena below, which might very occasionally occur. This is where the energy of the, up to now, invisible circle enclosing the ellipses takes over or overrides the energy of the ellipses (see diagram). Conversely it may be that the energy of emerging ellipses takes over or overrides the energy of the first information, shown in the form of a circle. This phenomenon is possible whether the circle is travelling in the same direction as the ellipses or not. Both patterns need translation when this occurs. It's just that the information is coming in faster than usual, and the second information is more dominant than the first. Ellipses dissolve into circles circles occasionally disolve into ellipses.

NOTE sometimes the pendulum will make some ellipses (daisy loops) and then decide to *continue by describing a circle travelling in the same direction.* A few daisy loops (travelling ellipses) are drawn, which would show you such things as the degree of effort required for a project (by how tightly packed the ellipses were) and then continue by drawing circles.

SPECIAL PHENOMENON DIAGRAM

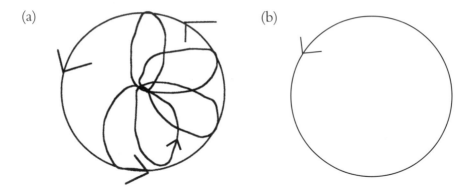

(a)　　　　　　　　　　(b)

NOTE In a HEALING context the size of any forward circles described is very important, because the forward circle is the WORKING/THINKING pattern and it means to me that some work is being done on the client by the guides. The situation will have been "opened up", the opportunity made, by the Healing energy of LOVE. (The pendulum swinging on the Love/ truth/ Healing /Gift line over this spot on the client's body.) This enables the GUIDES to move in. If the circles are of reasonable size the Healing is of a general nature, but if they become smaller it is a sign that the healing is becoming more concentrated and specific. I always tell my client when I see this concentration of energy happening and it is common for them to experience some healing phenomenon at this point. Quite often what they feel will be unusual to them. They may well say that they have never felt anything like it before, and often find it hard to describe.

POSITIVE AND NEGATIVE

Now let's look at the energy of the enclosing circle going forward in a positive direction but the energy of the individual ellipses going backwards, as shown below.

POSITIVE AND NEGATIVE DIAGRAM
positive circle, negative ellipses

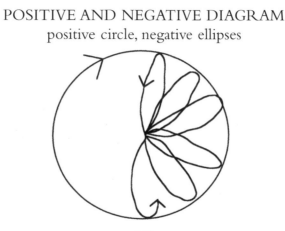

This is still "Pushing forward too fast" or "Pushing forward from a difficult place", but this time with an anticlockwise negative attitude, shown by the individual ellipses. For example, with concern, frustration, anger, hurt, depression, jealousy, resentment or a mixture of those emotions running at the same time.

NEGATIVE AND NEGATIVE

Next we have the enclosing circle energy going in an anticlockwise negative direction (Once again note that this circle as such is NOT SEEN) and the energy of the individual ellipses is ALSO negative and anticlockwise.

NEGATIVE AND NEGATIVE DIAGRAM
negative circle, negative ellipses

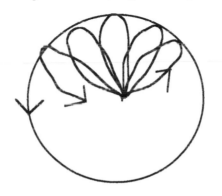

This pattern represents frantic or "boxed in" energy, (which is indicated by underlying axes of the ellipses and also the negative, anticlockwise direction of the outer circle,) with concern, frustration, anger, hurt, depression, jealousy, resentment, or a combination of those energies, as expressed through the anticlockwise movement by way of which the ellipses are "drawn." This is the most negative and potentially dangerous mind pattern I know, BOTH FOR THE PERSON THEMSELVES AND THOSE AROUND THEM.

Finally let us look at a negative circle pattern with a positive elliptical pattern.

NEGATIVE AND POSITIVE

Here we have a situation where the all-over energy for a situation is falling away, as expressed by the anticlockwise thrust of the ellipses as a whole, that is to say the outlining circle but it is countered by a positive energy direction in each individual ellipse. This positive energy may be interpreted by " If I can just keep going, I *can* win through. The going is tough, but I must keep positive and then it will be alright." Once again the WIDTH of the loops are indicative of effort, or how fast they are overcoming their difficulties. Generally speaking, with this sort of determination, the more tired a person gets, the harder they will drive themselves.

NEGATIVE AND POSITIVE DIAGRAM
negative circle, positive ellipses

Another pattern I quite often see is as illustrated below

ANTICLOCKWISE AXES, SETTLING ON THE TRUTH LINE

This is what I call ANXIOUS BUT OK. This means that although the person is feeling anxious, or worried about what is happening to themselves or to someone to whom the are close, they know in their heart of hearts that all is for the best and that the final outcome will be fine! The pendulum illustrates the anxious, or maybe even the Boxed In pattern, as shown, but then settles and remains on the line of Love, Truth and Healing. This pattern is often connected to the person's own sense of spirituality and their sense of support from the world of the Spirit.

ANTICLOCKWISE AXES, SETTLING ON THE TRUTH LINE DIAGRAM

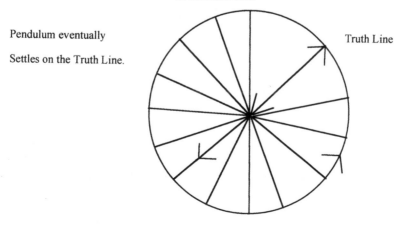

Pendulum eventually

Settles on the Truth Line.

Truth Line

One last phenomenon I would like to show you, which only appeared in chapter fourteen of this book, where I decided to give you an example of a Healing Session. This was a completely made-up scenario, or was it? The world of Spirit is not known for wasting energy and I saw a pattern on the pendulum in this "downloaded" example which I had not seen before. It occurred when I reached the point in the session where I was taking the energy reading of Jane's Deep Mind. Things that Jane might not even be clear on for herself.

I quote – "Here I see a certain boxed in pattern, but it settles on the Balance Line, in other words, and she confirms this when I challenge her with it, for I did get to realise who she was! She is in a situation she knows she can't get out of, but she also knows it is the will of God.

She has the reassurance that, for whatever reason, and this she cannot know, she is in the right place. It is her destiny and it is the will of God. What comfort there will be for Jane in this knowledge, coming as it does from such high authority!"

DIAGRAM OF BOXED IN PATTERN WHICH SETTLES ON THE BALANCE LINE

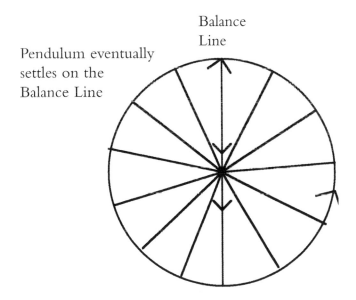

Balance
Line

Pendulum eventually
settles on the
Balance Line

Authors tip: Trace the lines of these pendulum language diagrams with the tip of your finger to accustom yourself to the movements involved.

Chapter Eleven

Recording Hieroglyphs

This chapter is all about how I am able to record my findings, through the swings of the pendulum, both quickly and easily, so that at a later date I could still recall and recount what insights had been received. These insights are recorded as they occur, in a duplicate book that I use for the purpose, the top sheet being offered to the client, while I retain the carbon copy for possible future reference.

Word	Hieroglyph
Balance	|
Yes	/
No	\\
Love, Truth, Gift, Healing	/
Fear, Pain Ignorance	\\
Obsession	/
Lethargy	\\

You can see that the angle at which the line is drawn is not geometrically accurate, but for this purpose of recording it does not have to be. You will soon recognise the different angles needed. If it concerns you then the balance line is vertical, the Yes and No lines are at an angle of 22.5 degrees to right and left, the Love and Fear lines are at 45 degrees to right and left and the Obsession and Lethargy lines are at 67.5 degree angles, to right and left.

Now let us look at how I record these same energies, with the addition of either a positive or negative aspect. The positive aspects are –

Thinking, Working, Learning, or Eternal/Always.

The negative aspects can be Irritation, Frustration, Concern, Anger, Hurt, Depression, Envy, Resentment or Sometimes. There may be a single word translation or the different moods may be combined to reach the truth of the situation, as confirmed by the Truth Line and, for example, the translation could be Anger and Frustration.

WORD	HIEROGLYPH showing positive energy	HIEROGLYPH showing negative energy
BALANCE/DIVINE CONNECTION		
YES		
NO		
LOVE TRUTH GIFT HEALING		
FEAR PAIN IGNORANCE		
OBSESSION		
LETHARGY		

Please remember, when studying these diagrams of positive and negative energy around the axes you do not see the axis or line, only the pendulum swinging in an elliptical shape in either a clockwise or anticlockwise direction. The size of the ellipse will of course vary from time to time according to how much energy is manifesting.

Word	Hieroglyph
Working Thinking Eternal/Always	
Pushing forward from a difficult place Pushing forward too fast	
Pushing forward from difficult place, possibly too fast, with Working/Thinking. The width of the loops are indicative of effort or time that may have elapse.	
Energy falling away for a project or situation. Boxed in, feeling hemmed in, trapped, not knowing how to get out of a situation or which route to take.	

125

WORD	HIEROGLYPH	HIEROGLYPH
Frustration, anger, irritation, hurt, depression, anxiety etc.		
Going forward, but feeling negative feelings.- Irritation, anger, frustration, etc	circle direction	plus ellipse direction
Trying hard to go forward, but with diminishing energy.		plus
Driving forward with Working/Thinking/Learning energy		plus
Boxed in, frantic energy, (underlying axes), plus frustration, anger etc. (ellipses).		plus
Anxious but never-the-less having an inner knowing that things will work out just fine.		settles on

| Name
Page 1 | Energies – All over
Pendulum | B | EM | SP | DM | OTHERS |
		Comments				Date
Fear Rock Rose						
Mimulus						
Cherry Plum						
Aspen						
Red Chestnut						
Uncertainty cerato						
Scleranthus						
Gentian						
Gorse						
Hornbeam						
Wild Oat						
Insufficient interest Clematis						
Honeysuckle						
Wild Rose						
Olive						
White chestnut						
Mustard						
Chestnut bud						
Loneliness Water violet						

Name

Page 1 Continuation	Pendulum	Comments	Date
Impatiens			
Heather			
Oversensitive to influences/Agrimony			
Centaury			
Walnut			
Holly			
Despondency/despair Larch			
Pine			
Elm			
Sweet chestnut			
Star of Bethehem			
Willow			
Oak			
Crab apple			
Over-care of others Chicory			
Vervain			
Vine			
Beech			
Rock water			

Chapter Twelve
Energies I am able to read from the aura

When a client comes to me for the first time I take some details on an index card, which will be kept in a small box file. These details are their given and their family name, for example, Jane and Brown. I file according to Christian names as these are what I always use. I introduce myself as Heather and then I say, " May I call you.........?" Then I take their postal address, telephone number, mobile number and possibly their e-mail address. This is in order that I have a means of contacting them to remind them of future appointments, or in case they had an appointment with me that I was unable to keep, or so I could send them information or a repeat prescription of their remedy. (Sometimes the bottle gets broken or knocked over, or they have been in such need of the Remedy that they have taken it rather often.) I also ask them to give me, in just a few words, the reason why they feel they need to see me. This is written on the card also. I keep the card out on the desk during this and every subsequent appointment, so that I can make reference to the different names of members of their family and special friends, or maybe those people whom they find specially difficult. I also make note of any medication they may be taking and assure them that there is no contra-indication to any medication for any of the Bach Flowers at any time, even in pregnancy.

It is also a good idea that when the person first makes contact, you note beside the booked appointment a contact telephone number for your client. It may also save wasting precious appointments if you ring to remind the client a day or two before they are due to see you.

BALANCE AND OVERALL ENERGY

Next I show how the pendulum starts to swing when I hold the word Balance in my mind. With a sheet of paper lying straight on the desk in front of me, the pendulum swings in a straight line towards the top and then towards the bottom of the sheet in a vertical line. This is the Balance line. When I first started working I next asked the pendulum to show me, by its swing, what the client's OVERALL energy reading was. This was the only energy reading I knew of at that time, but it is in fact the sum total of all their energies

I use notebooks with a duplicate sheet (12.5 x 20 centimetres) to note my findings and at the end of the session my client takes the original named and dated sheet of paper and I retain the copy, which remains in the notebook. I fill in the appropriate information section in the front of the book with name and date also. In that way I have my numbered reference material to hand and in a safe place, should we need to discuss it or refer to it later. Each page in the book has a number and the duplicate sheet has the same number. This comes into its own if I need to make up a repeat prescription, or if I have made up the remedies without my client being present, and mailed them. In this situation a Telephone Healing would probably follow, and the remedies given would also be discussed at such a time, so obviously I need to have the information to hand to be able to do that. Anything which shows your client evidence of your capability and friendly efficiency, is a great help in Healing, after all these people need to trust you as they are going to be sharing their most intimate thoughts, worries and concerns with you, so the client's name is duly written at the top of the paper, together with that day's date and the index in the front of the book is similarly filled in.

These days I am able to read far more than the Overall Energy. But I still take that one first by silently asking my guides to show me through the pendulum what that energy is. The following three energies that I read off my client's psyche are the Body Energy, the Everyday Mind Energy and the Spirit, or Spiritual Energy. We often hear Body Mind and Spirit referred to these days when talking holistically, as if that were the full extent of the matter, but actually it is not. Next follows the Deep Mind energy, the Soul Mind Energy, the Light Heart Energy, the Memory Mind, (both long term and short term memory), the Soul Energy, and, finally, (so far as I know, but the learning still continues) the Wisdom Mind Of course it is not always necessary to investigate all of these, certainly not in a single session. The fundamental four are, Body, Everyday Mind, Spiritual and Deep Mind Energies. I would always investigate these, plus any of the other named energies that my guides instructed me to. but if you are just starting out, be pleased if you can get a reading on the person's All over Energy. If I have been instructed by Spirit to look into any of the other energies there has always turned out to be a very good reason why it was necessary.

It is very important to take these readings as the whole purpose of the remedies is to counteract the imbalances found in the energetic systems, which also helps to bring about a situation closer to balance in a person's emotional life, and therefore facilitate healing. Helping us balance our reactions around such things as love, fear, compassion, jealousy etcetera is obviously important. However your mind, when dowsing, needs to be like a blank screen remember. The Energy and Remedy *connections* are only detected later. For example, let's say I found Lethargy in the Soul Mind and let's say that the pendulum later indicated the need for Elm (Bach Flower Remedy) as one of the remedies in the prescription. I would be able, through the pendulum giving me the Truth Line, to recognise that the Elm Remedy balanced the Lethargy Energy in the Soul Mind. This is helpful because I am always on the lookout for as much insight for my client as possible. INSIGHT PUSHES OUT FEAR/PAIN. Soul Mind is about what we PERCEIVE our connection with the Divine Energy to be, not what it IS. We have lethargy, tiredness, lack of effort showing itself. Elm's INDICATION (Negative aspect) is about doing good work and following our Life purpose and yet feeling overwhelmed by the task and feeling that it is not within our power, while the AFFIRMATION (Positive aspect) is like "psychological smelling salts". It lends strength to the strong in moments of weakness. If one can tie up the two energies of Elm and Lethargy like this the result is first very insightful and then very psychologically supportive over the next days and weeks. (By the way, the pendulum provided this complete example for you when I asked the guides to illustrate the point I was trying to make.) The "Indication" energies discovered (in this example, Lethargy) are recorded alongside the chosen remedy in terms of the hieroglyphs as shown in the previous chapter. The different Mind energies are recorded in a space under the person's name at the top of the page. If you preferred you could devise a pre-printed sheet for each client, so that you only need to fill in the relevant boxes. I show you at the end of chapter eleven the sort of thing I mean, but I have always used the directly written individual, 'Home-made for each client' approach as being less 'clinical' and more friendly. I am not a clinic as such here, but have long dedicated a room in my home to the purpose of Healing, because I get requests for my help so very frequently.

BODY ENERGY

The Body Energy is the energy, or lack of it, which is in the physical body. It may, for example be found to be on "Lethargy" or "Working/Thinking", always busy, or, maybe on the Fear/Pain line, (or just below it), which would mean that the person would have the feeling of pain somewhere in their physical body. This is most interesting because it shows the degree of negativity, (literally at least 45 degrees to the left of the vertical) that a person needs to experience before the emergence of the energy interpreted as physical pain in the body is possible. This would be a vital piece of information for anyone who is working to control pain, be it their own or someone else's, to be aware of. And yes, I can work on myself to some extent, but not fully like I can with other people. One reason for this is that I too have to be able to ask for help from another person. The humility and the ability to ask for help is fundamental, and Healers should all have someone whom they visit from time to time for a session.

EVERYDAY MIND ENERGY

Next we look at the Everyday Mind, which is exactly what it says it is; the upper levels of the conscious mind which we use all the time in going about our normal daily life. The energy reading on Everyday Mind may for example show anxiety. This would register first of all as an anticlockwise circle but you would then need to use your pendulum to go through the possible interpretations of that movement, until the pendulum gave you the Truth line. Remember that there could be more than one interpretation to form the whole Truth. Obviously these different interpretations may be discussed by you with the client as they come up and it needs to be explained to the client that it is good to talk to someone sympathetic and trustworthy, in safe circumstances. The talking out of problems is, in itself, part of the healing process. Technically it clears the blocked energy in the body's energetic systems. Do remember however that a pledge to confidentiality on your part is most important. This is why healers themselves need to have a competent person to clear possible accumulated negative energy "stuff" from time to time.

SPIRIT ENERGY

Now we come to Spirit Energy or, in a broad sense, Spiritual Energy. These are thought to be the corner stones of alternative medicine - Body Mind and Spirit. Spirit is the all-important extra ingredient that traditional medicine does not overtly address, but it is the area where we get in touch with who we truly are, and, I believe, the wisdom that we have learned over time, the experience of this and former lives. As I have spent years now as a Past Life Regression therapist as well as a Healer, I have very good evidence for saying this. To give you a general example of what I mean, when I have facilitated a regression with a client who has 'visited' more than one life in a single session, or I have regressed a client on more than one occasion, the more recent lives show spiritual and ethical progress. That is not to say that it would not be possible to be retrograde as well, but, working as I have been, with people directed to me by Spirit (they so often say, "I was definitely led here,") it has not been of my experience.

When I look into the energy of Spirit I am not concerned with religion or with what religious group my clients align themselves, if any. I do not decry spiritual support from an organised group. As you know, I belong to one myself, but this is not my concern here. Having explained the importance of a connection to the Divine Energy, I am required to see how weak or strong that connection is and how it can be strengthened, because strengthening it increases our chances of well-being! Research has shown that those of us who have a spiritual faith, believe in a higher power, are generally happier and live longer. This is not simply psychological. It does **actually affect the health of each**

individual cell in the body.

Having asked my guides to give me an example of someone's Spirit Energy reading for you, they have given me a pattern that means 'Just keep going , it will be alright.' If this had happened in a session with a client, I should say something like. "You don't feel very connected to the world of Spirit and a sense of your own spirituality. You would like to feel more in touch with things of this nature, but maybe you don't know how to go about it?" Then, as you already know, it is good to talk, and so I would hope the client could feel safe enough to talk their feelings out with me. Because I am constantly being fed information through the pendulum I am always able to have a constructive and interactive conversation with my client. Quite often the pendulum will be swinging away, mirroring the conversation and confirming information as we speak. This allows me to pick up on any deviation between its swings and what is being said and I explain that this is a three way discussion (the client, Spirit Helpers/Angels and myself). I often talk of the pendulum as my celestial telephone.

DEEP MIND ENERGY

Now we go deeper still, into the level of the subconscious, or possibly the unconscious mind, and when this reading is taken I explain that my client may well not be aware, because of its deepening nature, of what is going on there. There are two levels to Deep Mind, the Subconscious or half hidden and the Unconscious or hidden level. How do thoughts and feelings get trapped at these lower mind levels? They get there by being suppressed by the individual themselves. Perhaps the person feels that their feelings will not be well received, or that they are 'bad', or maybe that if they are expressed they may hurt someone else and so, instead of being expressed they are suppressed in situations like this, deeper than usual, until they are buried deep deep down and possibly even denied.

The Subconscious level can be brought up to the Everyday Mind level, by my client and I working in an honest and open way, starting with the energy reading. For example, say the pendulum showed Fear there in the Subconscious, then we would start looking for what that fear was about. Some examples might be suggested such as –

Fear of having another baby.

Fear of losing a job.

Fear of flying.

Being in the subconscious, my client would not have been sufficiently aware of the feeling to fully recognise the fear. The pendulum, (and for **pendulum** you can, if you prefer, read **intuition**) would help us find which of these examples among many possible others, was the correct one. Having named the fear it is easier to talk about and think through. The remedy would probably be simple and straightforward - **Mimulus**, one of the Bach flower essences, which helps us deal with fear of a known thing.

When the root cause of a problem is buried even deeper in the client's mind, it is still possible for me to read the energy which exists there. Why am I aware of what is in the client's mind when they are not? This is because of experience and training. I have explored Deep Mind through mystical and shamanic means. A Shaman is 'One who knows'; one who can read parts of the Akashic Records. It has been given to me and others like me, to simply know, or more accurately, to be instantly told. As I sometimes say, I am just the secretary taking notes from the boss. Next question, 'Who's the boss?' My reply, if I had to make one, would ultimately be the Divine Loving Creative Mind, a collective consciousness. People through the ages have been entrusted and continue to be entrusted with such knowledge because they have proved themselves to the world of Spirit to be worthy of that trust. They have used practices such as meditation, stillness and emptiness of mind to delve beneath the surface of the mind. They have looked beyond, to the source of their experiences, to the essence of the Unconscious, or One Consciousness, and have there found a profound connection with the Ground of all Being.

This professed establishment of a link to the Divine was deemed in the past to be heretical (Root meaning - 'One who is able to choose'. Latin - haeresis - choice,) and blasphemous. When the fourteenth century German mystic Meister Erkhart preached, " God and I are One," he was brought before the Pope of the day and made to "recant everything that he had falsely taught". Many mystics in the past have been martyred for using language which claimed unity with God.

However I can only be honest with you and say what I believe to be true, which is that we all have the propensity for direct contact to the Divine Mind, without the need for a human intermediary, if we work to establish the link. It is as if I am permitted to bring back from the place where all things are known certain information, which is going to enable those who ask for help to be helped, not so much by me as through me. It is a very important thing for us all to have the humility to be able to ask for help

An example of what might be found in the deep mind could be the pendulum swinging on the "Yes" line and then on the "No" line repeatedly.(Yes /No/ Yes/No) This you will see represents indecision. We would then address indecision and try to decipher together what was causing it. It's like being a psychic detective and you have always to be alert and looking for clues.

I could find such patterns as Fear or Working /Thinking in the Deep Mind. Remember, to be experiencing these energies would be very draining, to be constantly experiencing a state of fear, or have your mind never having a chance to rest. The brain may be technically in a state of sleep but the mind is still fully active, yet the person themselves is not consciously aware of what is going on!

Let's take the example of Fear being found. We would then talk around the subject and try to establish what the unconscious fear is about. Remember Insight pushes out Fear and pain and the whole aim is to address issues rather than denying them or hiding them away. That way they can be processed and released. If they cannot be retrieved in this way, then regression techniques are probably called for.

God was traditionally needed to fill the gaps in human knowledge, to explain what we could not explain. Modern science having explored deeply into the realms of space, time and matter, often appears to be able to dispense with God. Nowhere does science, of itself, declare finding evidence for God. As far as most scientists are concerned the universe seems to work perfectly well without Divine assistance. Conversely, to a believer, evidence of the Divine is everywhere.

God has long been thought of as the God of the Gaps, but as more and more things were discovered, the Divine was driven back, so to speak, into a smaller and smaller area of the unknown. Of course the scientists, if they are looking at all, are looking for the Divine, I humbly suggest, in a somewhat inappropriate place. The most convincing evidence for its existence is in the metaphysical realm, where the world of Academia has little part, where intuition comes first and left brain learning takes second place, where things sometimes must be taken on trust and may not necessarily be proved. This is the world of the mystic. and here God, the Divine Energy, is **still** the God of the Gaps; The Universal Mind fills in gaps in our knowledge, explains things we cannot explain, no longer esoterically but openly, physically, in our own personal physical experience, when the **TIME IS RIGHT**, and we are deemed ready. The brief of science is to gain knowledge through careful observation of the natural world. This knowledge is tested and retested in very carefully monitored, controlled situations so that the same results are repeatedly obtained. However the ability of the pendulum to repeatedly produce precisely accurate client information of which I am not previously aware and even they may not have been fully aware, concerning their thoughts feelings and emotions, this happening in carefully monitored controlled situations, is still, after all these years, truly amazing to me. All this is happening not just every once in a while but on an almost daily basis. God is indeed God of the Gaps, but they are gaps of which the scientist, with his scientist's hat on, is not aware.

I have often noticed blocks in a person's energy be cleared away simply because they could become accurately aware of their problems, being able to cross check on the pendulum what those problems were and having an opportunity to talk to an understanding person about them. Of course you, yourself, will have helped heal many people in the past by listening to them and trying to understand them. It's just that with the insights I get I can take it all just that bit further, and I am able to show you how you can do that too.

This concludes the four energies that I always address with each client, and it is important to note that the Bach flowers you will learn to choose will, in terms of their energy as well as their meaning, and the insights they will therefore afford, have the capacity to deal with the problems and difficulties found.

PART TWO (Advanced)

There are, however, other energies that I sometimes need to address. This section you might feel like leaving for a time, until you have practised reading and working with the first four energies listed and feel competent with the first part of this chapter.

SOUL MIND ENERGY

The next energy that I might be asked by my guides to look at would be what I call Soul Mind Energy. This is not concerned with the Divine link with us, which is always there. We are all known, loved and understood, even though the love may sometimes be tough love and we get, not what we want, but rather what we need. We are constantly encouraged to take up challenges and make progress. This life is indeed a schoolroom. Jesus Christ, in the gnostic gospel, Pistis Sophia, is quoted as saying "Souls are poured from one into another of different bodies of the world."   My personal experience is that it is true that every last thing about us is known, seen and understood because our soul's journey has been recorded by an Energy Form who may be thought of as the Keeper of the Records, and stored in our Book of Life, which contains the complete life histories of every personality we have ever emanated. This is why replaying the script and acknowledging the error, **healing and regression**, mends problems of the soul.

Soul Mind energy, in general terms, is about what we **perceive** our connection to the Divine Source to be. The healing of the soul is an area which does sometimes require Regression work (Far Mind investigation) to be done. The only way the therapist can get deep enough into the mind of the client safely is for them to be put into an altered state of consciousness, a bit like a traditional surgeon putting a patient under anaesthetic, so that they can literally relive and usually, although not always, remember their experiences in another time and place, without all the protracted pain. The regression process brings these very deep traumas up into the Every Day Mind of this life where they are processed and released. Once again, wisdom, understanding and insight pushes out fear, ignorance and pain and thus mends the current Soul Mind situation.

Leaving the subject of regression for the moment, as that is another whole book in itself, let's get back to talking about a more usual Healing session, where some different examples of possible energies found in the Soul Mind could be:

Fear - maybe through not being able to cope with the idea of an all seeing all knowing Intelligence.

Lethargy - laziness, holding back, never having done much work on the subject.

Positive - pendulum making a clockwise ellipse around the Yes line, which shows an impetus, or willingness to go forward. Interested, open, wanting to learn more.

It could be most helpful to be made aware of these energies, both from the point of view of the client and also from my point of view, as one who is trying to free the client up and enable them to go forward on their journey towards enlightenment. Also remember, if there was a problem in this Energy, there would be a corresponding Flower Essence which would support the correction of the error esoterically (secretly) as well as the person, having been made more aware, being able to work on the problem consciously.

Of course the ultimate healing of the Soul Mind that is possible on this level of existence takes place in a regression session. Regression therapy is able to deal with both Far Mind and Soul Mind trauma, but it must be said that it demands of its practitioners a high degree of patience, intuition and technical virtuosity. Here the client is eased into a relaxed and altered state of consciousness in order to remember happenings which have occurred in another time and place. This is where the Divine, God of the Gaps, provides infills in the client's remembering, putting memories back together again, making the information more complete. This is the compassionate act of a loving and caring consciousness which knows everything there is to know about us and wishes us to be complete and functioning fully. That way we can play our part in helping make even the wheels of the universe go around.

LIGHT HEART ENERGY

The next energy that may be investigated is named Light Heart Energy. Someone whom I respect very much once told me that the heart is older than the soul. I believe this could well be true. If Love is the source of all creation, only after the creative experience of Love would the Memory Bank/Soul evolve in which to store those experiences. In the Dionysis system of angels, the Seraphim are said to be closest to the Divine source, which is pure Love. They send out energy waves of Love from the Source, in the form of movement, colour and sound, which can be experienced by all sentient (feeling) beings, including the Standing Ones or plant beings.

Some time ago, in a magazine called 'Living Lightly', which is published under the auspices of Positive News, Virginia Kennedy wrote an article called 'The Intelligence of the Heart.' In it she says, " It is not just the love struck and poets who allude to the heart as the seat of their emotions. We put our 'heart' into our work, take criticism 'to heart', make 'heartfelt' pleas or are 'hard hearted'."

Western medicine however treats the heart as a pump for pumping blood around the body; to the lungs for oxygenation and thence to the rest of the body, so is there any conjoining between these opposing points of view?

To quote Virginia Kennedy again, "In the laboratory scientists have discovered that when subjects focus on the area of the heart and initiate core heart feeling such as love, appreciation or care, this alters heart rhythms. When these rhythms become more coherent. there is a cascade of neural and biochemical events which affects almost every system and organ of the body. There is a reduction in the level of the stress hormone cortisol, an increased level of IgA - an important antibody in the body's immune system, improved brain function, lower blood pressure, and, of course, a sensation of well being, both mentally and emotionally."

"In recent years neuroscientists have discovered that the heart has its own independent nervous system. The heart's intrinsic "brain" and nervous system relay information back to the brain in the cranium, creating a two way communication system. The signals sent from the heart to the brain have been found to affect many areas and functions in the amygdala, the thalamus and the cortex. The amygdala is an almond-shaped structure deep inside the brain's emotional processing system which specialises in strong emotional memories. The cortex is where learning and reasoning occur, including problem solving and determining right from wrong."

From the same article I quote " In his book 'Teaching children to love" Doc Childre states:

"Within our brain is a dramatically distinctive 'emotional cognitive' structure which functions as a veritable command centre for our mind-body system. It is this centre of the brain which is linked to our heart through direct neural and hormonal connections and is subject to a heart- centred electromagnetic field 40 to 60 times more powerful in amplitude than the brain's own electrical output. This heart – brain dynamic modulates and regulates every function of the body and the brain, influences our endocrine glandular functions, immune system, capacity for body healing, all memory and learning, DNA activity, and of course all relationships."

The initials DNA stand for Deoxyribonic acids, which are nucleic acids containing deoxyribose (sugar) and consisting of complex molecules present in chromosomes of all plant and animal cells, carrying, in coded form, instructions for passing on of hereditary characteristics.

The initials RNA stand for Ribonucleic acids, which are nucleic acids containing ribose, present in living cells, where they play an important part in the development of proteins.

Ribose is a pentose. Riboflavin, from the Latin flavus - yellow, is a member of the vitamin B complex. RNA is connected to the nucleus of the cell. Nucleus is a central mass or kernel, and the origin of the word is from the Latin, nux, nucis - a nut.

The nucleic acids are informational molecules because their primary structure contains a code or set of directions by which they can duplicate themselves and guide the synthesis of proteins. The synthesis of proteins, most of which are enzymes, ultimately governs the metabolic activities of the cell. In 1953, Watson, an American biologist, and Crick, an English biologist, proposed the double helix structure for DNA. This development set the stage for a new and continuing era of chemical and biological investigation. The two main events in the life of a cell - dividing to make exact copies of themselves, and manufacturing proteins - both rely on blueprints coded in our genes.

So - What of Light Heart Energy? Well, maybe you can now see why a lightness of heart is important to well-being, why I would need, if the person was heavy hearted, to see how far the energy here was out of balance, what the contributory factors were and what remedial remedies were necessary to help put the matter right. Remedial measures may include regression, which has the power to change RNA and even DNA structures, especially where psychic surgery is employed. This could be a vital Healing tool in the future, especially if children or those just developing a debilitating disease (dis - ease) could be so treated in the early stages of development of that disease.

LONG TERM MEMORY MIND   FAR MEMORY MIND

As you already realise, sometimes people can store memories from long, long ago, even from another lifetime (FAR MEMORY.) These may well not be memories of which they are generally consciously aware, but could emerge now and then, in dreams or in times of quiet rest, perhaps while on the edge of sleep.

In Regression situations, people are sometimes even able, for example, to remember what it felt like to be in the womb. However, in a regular Healing session, (not a regression session) what I am more likely to be dealing with are post-birth memories from this lifetime. It is however sometimes necessary to uncover these 'present life' memories, when the person feels ready to do so, in 'This Life' regression therapy as they have been erased, because of their difficult nature, from the person's LONG TERM MEMORY MIND and are then only recoverable from the FAR MEMORY MIND.

Correspondingly sometimes memories from long ago can be too *dominant* and we find ourselves too caught up with how things used to be. This could happen for example in a grief situation, when the person is still hankering after the "old" life instead of living in the present. This is, to some extent inevitable for a while, but it should not carry on too long, or it will be detrimental to health and well-being. You may remember me saying that one of the most important things for well-being is to be in the Now, to live in the moment. **Honeysuckle** is a very good remedy for helping us move on in our lives and leave the past behind, but if grief itself was actually the problem, some **Star of Bethlehem** taken for a while is a wonderful remedy for consolation.

SHORT TERM MEMORY MIND

It is said that as we get older we often find it easier to remember what happened twenty years ago than to remember what happened yesterday. Of course this can be alarming and people start to worry about degenerative diseases like senile dementia and Alzheimer's disease. There are precautions we can take. There are many books available which will help you with good advice on minimising the risk of these problems, but, in general terms I would like to share these few thoughts with you. It is good to reduce the intake of stimulants such as tea, coffee, chocolate, alcohol, cola and highly sweetened drinks. Minimise intake of fat and sugar in all forms. Try to minimise your exposure to pollution and cigarette smoke. Make sure you include some nuts and seeds in your diet on a daily basis. Try to eat a little wholemeal bread and some unrefined cereal, particularly oats for the heart, each day. Use fresh unprocessed meats, fish, eggs, vegetables and fruit in your diet, steamed or cooked with the minimum of fat. Instead, if necessary, use a little olive oil of the type which has been specially prepared for cooking. Drink plenty of fresh water each day. Taking a good multivitamin tablet each day is likely to be a good idea. Taking advantage of the regular checks offered by doctors and dentists is important also. Mentally we need to be stimulated and to remain alert and alive to the possibilities of each day. Hobbies, shared interest groups, adult education classes and social gatherings all help to keep us mentally healthy. Each day of your life starts as a blank page. It is up to you what you choose to write on that page, but what you don't put into life, you don't get out.

SOUL ENERGY

This energy is concerned with the receiving and passing on of Love, in order that there is a continuous flow of this wonderful energy passing through us all the time. When I am working with a client on LOVE energy I divide it, first of all into their ability to give it and then their ability to receive it. You will understand, I am sure that some of us are better at giving than we are at receiving, while for others it is the other way around; they are better at receiving than giving. That in itself can be a helpful insight to look at and discuss. Many of us find it difficult to be loved and many find it difficult to be loving. For some these emotional problems can be the result of long term damage, while for others they may be much more short term, more to do with the mood of the day, or even the moment. Further insights can be gained when you have discovered by dowsing which remedy it is which counteracts the negative energy uncovered.

Let's say for example that someone has a problem, long term, with receiving love, allowing themselves to be loved. It may be discovered that the Remedy necessary is coming from the group or nosode, "For the over-care for the welfare of others." Let us now suppose that the remedy the pendulum has chosen is Vine. The Principle of Vine is that it relates to the soul potential of authority and ability to carry conviction. A person in the negative Vine state may be hard, greedy for power, with no respect for the individuality of others.

To quote from the extremely helpful book by Mechthild Scheffer "Bach Flower therapy   the complete approach" - This is the sentence that the pendulum has indicated through the Love, Truth, healing Line for our imaginary client.

" When we take Vine, opening up to our Higher Self and to the higher goals of the soul, we will realise that we are supported by the very power that we were trying to use to gain control over everything before. We will feel how willpower unites with love, and strength with wisdom."

Once again, my guides have just provided me with this example, in order that I share my way of working with you. You can see, I am sure, how helpful this degree of insight is to the client because the error is clearly identified. Also, of course, the remedy works on the client's energy and energy field esoterically, in order to bring about the conditions necessary for correction.

You may be finding these examples difficult or tedious to follow at the moment, but please continue to read on as they are intended to show you the great benefits to be gained in the long term through your determined persistence in learning the language of pendulum movement. Suddenly the mist of doubt about your abilities in all this will clear, I promise you, if you can just "Hang on in there" and persevere! (Or drop the book and do something completely different, which is often an excellent idea, and allows you to approach the difficulty afresh another day!)

Now to explore a second example, one around the issue of the ability to give love. This is an example when there is an emotional mood swing, as illustrated to me by the pendulum swinging first to one side and then to the other of the Balance line. (Yes and No) Sometimes they can and sometimes they can't give out love. The remedy, I'm told, by the pendulum swinging on the Truth line over the " For Loneliness" group (page 16 of the little booklet, "The Twelve Healers" written by Edward Bach, is in the group or nosode "Loneliness", and the remedy identified is Heather. Why?

" The principle of Heather is that it relates to the soul qualities of empathy and readiness to help. In the negative state one is only concerned with oneself and one's own problems, and may be even trying to solve them at the cost of others. This state may be of either the extrovert or introvert type."

In our example the client is swinging from positive to negative states and back again. The flow of love energy, however is only being blocked in the negative state, as spoken of above and so you can see that sometimes they would be able to give love, but only when in the positive, helpful, supportive state and not when wrapped up in their own affairs. The insight to the client would of course be most helpful to them, but also the remedy would support them energetically at all times, while they continue to take it.

WISDOM MIND

"Where ignorance is bliss, 'tis a folly to be wise." This can certainly be true in the short term. It is as well that we remain blissfully unaware, for the most part, of what lies around the next corner, whether it be perceived as "good" or "bad", as to know the future before it arrives would influence us too much. However WISDOM MIND is not really about the wisdom stored in our own souls, but about our permission, or rite of passage to link with other souls as a collective and share their wisdom, as if being of one soul. The Tibetans call this Dzogchen.

"NO ONE CAN DIE FEARLESSLY and in complete security until they have truly realised the nature of mind", says Sogyal Rinpoche in his book "The Tibetan Book of Living and Dying". (ISBN 0-7126-1569-5) The origins of Dzogchen are, he says, traced to the Primordial Buddha, Samantabhadra, from whom it has been handed down in an unbroken line of great masters to the present. Dzogchen, he continues, is not simply a teaching, not another philosophy, not a seductive clutch of techniques. Dzogchen is a state, *the* primordial state, that state of total awakening that is the heart essence of all the buddhas and all spiritual paths, and the summit of the individual's spiritual evolution. The Ground of Dzogchen is this fundamental primordial state, our Absolute nature which is already perfect and always present. Yet, we have to understand, the buddhas took one path and we took another. The buddhas recognise their original nature and become enlightened; we do not recognise that nature and so become confused. Finally, to recognise our original nature is to attain complete liberation and become a buddha. This is the Fruition of Dzogchen and is actually possible, (if a practitioner really puts his or her heart and mind to it) in one lifetime.

Chapter Thirteen

My experiences with the
Bach Flower Remedies
Hands on Healing

As a result of personal experience, I know that the remedies can be used with people or animals, or indeed plants, of any age or condition of health, and that the appropriate remedies can be detected through the pendulum, ideally, but not necessarily when in my subject's presence. The information being picked up is not coming from the subject themselves but through guides who are in possession of information about the innermost thoughts, experiences and workings of the mind as recorded in the akashic record of that subject.

All this poses the very interesting problem of plants. Does it mean that at some basic level plants have feelings, which vary from individual plant to plant, not merely from type to type, as well as an ability to "think"? I believe it does. If I can work through thirty eight different states of mind and come up with maybe three or four remedies which refer to different states of mind, and these remedies, when applied to the plant, in solution with water, lead to it's return to good health, then to me this is indicative of at least *something* going on!

I remember many years ago first finding out that the Bach Flowers work with plants. I had a plant on my landing windowsill which was failing badly. It was a syngonium or goose foot plant, quite a strident and vigourous plant, but definitely in decline and many of its leaves had gone from bright green to yellow. Some of the yellow leaves even had dry brown parchment like patches on them. I decided to dowse in order to try and find out what was going wrong. The four remedies I discovered were Hornbeam, Walnut, Heather and gorse. Hornbeam was because every day was an uphill struggle, Walnut was to support change – the plant had recently been moved from a group of plants in the lounge to its lone place on the windowsill, which was also why it needed Heather, because it was feeling lonely, and finally Gorse because it had almost given up hope that anything could be done to save its life! All this although it had, up to this time, done well and been reasonably well looked after. Then I watered my plant with water containing two drops each of the four remedies in a small watering can. The result was extraordinary! Within thirty-six hours all the yellow leaves had gone back to green again. Obviously the little brown areas which were past recovery could not be changed. They were dead and that was that, but everything else perked up amazingly and I have the plant still!

A good way to detect just one highly significant remedy if you do not have much experience, or if there is not much time to spare and yet you would still like to help a friend, their animal, or a client in a very real and practical way, is to initially work through the seven groups or nosodes at the beginning of the small paperback book, The Twelve Healers, written by Edward Bach, which I still use constantly. The pendulum is highly likely to pick out one of these groups, rejecting the others. It will pick out the particular group by swinging on the Yes Line if you only have experience with Yes or No positions, or the Truth/Healing Line, if you are already familiar with it. You then turn to that particular section in the book and test each remedy in turn, until only one remedy is picked out, again by the indication of either the Yes Line or the Truth line. So you see, in two simple actions you have discovered just one very highly significant remedy out of the thirty eight possible ones. Quick and simple!

Having discovered the energy requirements of my subject, be it human, plant or animal, as far as the Bach flowers are concerned, we then have to decide the best method of administration.

Administration could be by mouth and this would most usually be the case. Remembering that as the flower essences are a very subtle form of homeopathy, ideally they should be taken a minimum of thirty minutes away from digestion, from taking anything to eat or drink, and ideally in a little water to aid their assimilation. However we do not live in an ideal world and, as I say, the remedies work better in the body than they do in the bottle, so I realise that, in fact, they are often administered directly from the treatment bottle that I dispense, into the client's mouth. If this is in fact the case, then great care should be taken to avoid touching any part of the mouth with the pipette, as this part could, in that way, become contaminated and so go on to contaminate the whole of the treatment bottle. Remedies are taken at least four times a day, first thing on waking, mid afternoon, mid evening and again last thing before retiring to bed for example, and I often suggest at the commencement of treatment, that another dose is taken mid morning, making five times in all. They can be taken, however, as often as felt necessary, but the number of drops is always the same. There is absolutely no advantage in 'doubling up' as in traditional medicine. In fact if you took the whole bottle at once it would still only have the effect of one dose, so it is impossible to overdose.

The dispensing method with animals depends on the relationship of owner to animal. Most animals I have had the pleasure to work with are domesticated and seem very accepting of this form of help from those they have learned to love and trust. As such they are very ready to take the remedy directly from the dropper of the prepared treatment bottle. The animal's mouth is merely opened and the drops administered, being careful, of course, not to allow the glass pipette itself to make contact. If taking the remedy directly by mouth proves difficult it can be dropped onto food, into their drinking water, which should be replaced daily, or onto soft tissue points on the animal's body and gently massaged in. A loving act such as this would help, if found to be acceptable to the animal, because as you recall, it is the Love energy that heals.

I have another friend of many years who is a farmer. He is an excellent custodian of his animals and occasionally he will express a concern about a certain group of livestock in his care. I dowse for a single remedy by picking out a group or nosode from the front of the little "Twelve Healers" booklet and then picking out one remedy from that group. This remedy will be put into the animals' water trough straight from the stock bottle, usually ten drops to a trough, to very beneficial effect. But now, after the publication of this book, he will be able to work out the solution for himself! I also have a friend who owns cats. She solves the problem by spraying the remedy from a little spray bottle onto the cats' paws.

Some while ago there was an article published in Positive News called " The Healing Power of Flowers", by Clare G Harvey. In this article she says, "Orthodox medicine offers little in the way to relieve stress induced turbulence. Drugs such as tranquillisers may ease the discomfort by dulling our perceptions and reactions, but they do not really help us stay afloat in this sea of turmoil. This is where flower remedies come to our rescue.

Flower essences are not like other medicines, They do not contain active chemicals or possess pharmaceutical properties. They are best described as a sort of liquid energy, a vibrational medicine that brings about benefits by influencing each person's (author's insert – living thing's) own life-force."

Let us never forget in this technocratic age that WE OURSELVES need to retain the power of personal responsibility FOR OURSELVES. Too many people are telling us, not merely advising us, what we should be doing. Here let me share with you the four reliances that the Buddha taught –

1 Rely on the message of the teacher, not on his (or her) personality.
2 Rely on the meaning, not just on the words.
3 Rely on the real meaning , not on the provisional one.
4 Rely on your wisdom mind and not on your ordinary judgemental mind.

Besides taking the remedies by mouth as we have already spoken about, they may be applied to the body in their Stock Bottle strength, as they come from the shop, or more usually in their Treatment bottle strength, as made up according to instructions, by yourself or your practitioner. To give you an example of when this may need to occur:

You have just sprained your ankle by falling in the street. You are prudent enough to be carrying a spraybottle of Rescue Remedy with you. You might well decide to not only take four drops by mouth immediately to calm yourself down, but also to spray some of the liquid into a cupped hand and apply direct to the injury site. An even better help might be to spray some Rescue Remedy on to a hankie and bind it around the injury site.

I realised long ago that it could be beneficial to apply the remedies to the body as well as to take them by mouth, and at first I used to dowse for the remedies required. Then I came upon the wonderful work of Dietmar Kramer and Helmut Wild in the book entitled 'New Bach flower Body Maps – Treatment by Topical Application.' Now I work with my client, by means of the body maps, to identify the areas of pain and strain in their body and follow the recommendations of these two amazing people. I usually to put eight drops of each of the chosen remedies into 50 ml bottles of almond oil, adding not more than four different remedies to each bottle. The bottle needs to be shaken prior to use each time in order to thoroughly mix the oil and water contents, and a little is gently applied at least twice a day, morning and evening, to the area of pain, but can be applied more often, as required.

You may be thinking that if there are specific areas in the body requiring specific remedies, how is it possible that I am able to combine as many as four remedies in the one bottle? This is because the body only takes in, when allowed to work in this Energetic way, what it needs and not what it does not. Therefore any remedy applied to an area not needing that particular remedy will simply not be affected by it. Similarly, do not worry when initially dispensing remedies for people to take by mouth. If the Energetic body does not need a certain remedy, that remedy will simply not be affective.

You may also be wondering why so little of the remedy can bring about such amazing results. Certainly one of the reasons for this is the capacity of both the water and oil carriers to effectively memorise the flower remedy energy incorporated into them. As you now know, The Thought is The Deed. From this point of view, if no other means of getting a remedy to someone is open to you, then you can use the power of positive thought.

If, for example, you felt that someone you knew was being particularly critical and intolerant, (and, of course you would need to check carefully that you were justified in your opinion,) then it might be possible to ameliorate the situation by sending them some Beech remedy by the power of your conscious thought and deed. You could do this by writing the person's name on a little card and writing the name of the chosen remedy, in this case Beech, underneath it. Beech is for tolerance, lenience and understanding of the way all things are working towards their final perfection. Be sure to do this work in the name of the Divine Beloved Energy of course and not to any particular agenda of your own.

Occasionally I have had clients, who for one reason or another are not able to take the remedies by mouth. This need not be a problem as **Intention** is fundamentally important. For example, you could write the remedies on a card and the person could carry the card around in their pocket or purse and that would work. Another way would be to write the remedies on a card and place the card under a glass of water, in order that the power of the words potentise the water. The person then sips from the glass of water during the day, making up a fresh glass each day. These remedies are capable of working on very subtle levels and the thought is the deed.

I was working with a friend of mine recently who was having a very serious operation in America for a brain tumour. I had recommended, as I always do, that she take Rescue Remedy for two or three days before the operation and two or three days after, in order to keep her energies better in balance and to minimise the possibility of post operative trauma. Her consultant would not hear of it. "No way! Absolutely no way!", was the reply given. "Have you any idea how good this stuff is?" my friend countered. " No, and that's the trouble." was the reply. The only way left open to me was to write the words RESCUE REMEDY on her Healing tabulation when she ran into serious difficulties post operatively.

It worked a treat, or at least something did! Of course, you can't work like this as a cheap shortcut. If you can obtain the actual Remedies then you must, but it certainly has always worked for me if there is no other way.

POSITIONS TO CHECK WHEN HEALING

This may be a good point at which to give you some advice on healing. As I have already said, I find the negative energy points on my client's body by the use of the pendulum, watching my pendulum, held in my right hand, while using the index finger of my left hand as a pointer, but it will take you a little while, maybe, to become proficient at this.

I have had a great deal of practice on thousands of people, but I *do* find that there are frequently recurring positions that crop up time and again, so I propose to give you a helpful checklist or two, or three, or four! The point I am making is that there is no one correct way. **Healing is not like that. You cannot learn it and know it and practice it and get slick and continue in the same way for ever more**. Every person is different, every session is different, every remedy is different and every hands on healing is different. What I **have learned** is that I simply turn up for work with an open heart and mind, and the **intention to help**. I do what my intuition tells me, and whatever happens, as a result, happens. That way, the person gets what they came for, and I don't burn out! You cannot learn your way through this, you have to **feel your way through, respond**, (re-back spondere, Latin- to promise.) If you sincerely, without guile, want to help, then the promise is with the angels and beings of light. They will respond. There is no way you can do this work, any of it, on your own.

The person is lying on their backs fully clothed in comfortable clothing, wearing nothing too baggy, shoes but not socks removed. Make sure they do not have bulky things like bunches of keys or purses or wallets in their pockets. Mobile phones have also been placed on the table in the "off" position. Spectacles are likewise removed. Personal jewellery, unless very bulky, is almost always fine, for me, but I **do** like watches removed. I work without a watch, and remove my shoes, to be in touch with the ground.

Taking the area where you might expect to use your red stone first, the Root Chakra, I would like you to check: (numbers 1-6 root chakra)
1. The soles of the feet. This can be a very powerful area for healing as it is here that we find representation for all the organs in the body.
2. The tops of the feet.
3. A point about eight centimetres up from the ankles.
4. The knees.
5. A point about twelve/fifteen centimetres down from the base of the spine on both legs
6. The right and left hips.
8. ADVANCED if you suspect psychic invasion, some negative outside energy force having invaded, check the energy on the inside and outside leg on both the right and left side, See last paragraph in this chapter.)

Taking the area where you might expect to use your orange stone, check right side, left side and central point of the Sacral Chakra. I usually work at a point roughly two thirds of the way up between hips and waist.

The Solar Plexus point (about fifteen centimetres up from the tummy button) is where you would expect to use your yellow stone, if you picked up negative energy.

The Heart Chakra is the next point you check, and here you may expect to use crystals of a pink or green colour. Keep to the centre of the body. The chakra positions are traditionally linked to the spine remember.

The Thymus is a position mid way between the heart and the throat. Use any of the four crystals here that were recommended in the tabulation included in chapter nine. (They were Turquoise, Chrysocolla, Angelite or Pale Jade.)

Having reached the shoulder area, I always check there and come down each arm. I would like you to learn to do this too, stopping off at a point about eight centimetres down from the shoulder, the elbows, eight centimetres up from the wrists, the wrists themselves and the centre points of the backs of the hands.

Our hands are what we work with, and so the energy reading here can be very insightful.

Always ask your client to put their hands down by their sides before you commence the healing. You may have given them a Master Crystal to hold, and this they would do by laying their hand, either right or left as instructed, over it.

When checking the Throat chakra, I always check the right and left sides of the throat also. This is where you would use one of your blue stones.

Next comes the Third Eye, about midway up the forehead, although I often found the point at which I must lay my crystal to be almost up to the hair line. I believe this is the sign of a more advanced soul. Use any recommendation for third eye crystals here. At this point I also check the right and left temple areas also, and right and left cheeks, when my client often get a feeling of warmth, like pleasant summer sunshine. You will find as you progress up the body your client will be becoming more and more relaxed.

Finally the Crown Chakra. As I have said before, but it's worth repeating, the crown is a very sensitive area and you could be a healer of some considerable experience before you feel ready to physically touch this point on your client. Therefore place both your choice of crystal and your healing hand a short distance *above your client's head.* Let's say ten centimetres for safety.

Now it is necessary for you to audibly make a previously decided upon, affirmation ending in either 'Amen' or 'So be it,' if that feels more comfortable for you. This is in order to close both yourself and your client down safely.

At this point you would take each crystal you have used in the healing separately, and ask if there is a message for your client in it. It is possible for you to check in this book, (Chapter Nine) to see, with the aid of your pendulum what that message might be. To check for a message from the client's guide, pass your pendulum **slowly** down over the relevant information about the crystal, and watch where your pendulum goes to the **Truth Line.** Do however, consider getting yourself a copy of the excellent reference book 'Love is in the Earth,' written by Melody, details to be found in the bibliography in this book.

Always wash your hands up to and including the wrists after healing. Also drink plenty of water, and advise your client to do likewise. Also rest and relaxation is important for both of you. Please note that I have listed different levels of difficulty in 'hands on healing' in this book. Use the level you feel most comfortable with:

1   Client in a chair. You have your hand(s) above their head.
2   Described above
3 & 4 Illustrated on the Energy Clearing Chart.

ADVANCED. If you suspected psychic invasion had occurred you would check the energy meridians up both the right and left leg, both inside and

My energy clearing chart (Advanced)

For Simple clearing use numbers 1. 4. 7. 8. 9. 10. 11. 18. 20.

crown 20

third eye 18   temples 17

cheeks right and left 16

throat 11

thymus 10

heart 9

Right and left brain 19

Shoulders 12

plexus 8

Sacral right and left 7

hips 6

About 12 - 15 cms down from top of leg. 5

knees 4

about 8cms up from ankle 3

tops of feet 2

soles of feet 1

Elbows 13

just above wrist 14
backs of hands 15

This clearing
is carried out
with client lying
on a bed, on
their backs,
wearing, if
possible, loose
comfortable
clothing.

outside. If you found evidence of negative energy there, which made you suspicious, you could gently introduce the subject, by asking if the person felt any serious negative influences around them which they wished to discuss. Had they had any really difficult dealings with someone who had recently died or unresolved problems with someone who was now in Spirit. Remember also to ask the opinion of your guide on this subject, through the pendulum. Simply ask silently, in your head, "Is this person affected by psychic invasion?" Your guide IS there to help you remember.

Soul Rescue and Exorcism is always a job for a trained professional, and no way should you attempt to deal with this yourself, unless you have received proper training, but helping your client by discussing the possibility of such a problem and guiding them to someone in your area who might be able to assist, is of course useful. You may be the only person to realise the potential problem exists.

Soul rescue and exorcism are areas in which I have worked. I didn't seek it out, it sought me. Remember the reason behind this would be that the person in spirit would be seeking help, just as the person in incarnation is. They will have a sense of who can help them release their negative tendencies and go forward into the light.

This is very unlikely to cause you any difficulty at all. You simply refer them to the person in your area who can help, but if you **should** be suddenly faced by a dark energy, and they **do** exist, be prepared. Have a spiritual text learned by heart, something like the Lord's Prayer or the Twenty third psalm, which you would repeat out loud as many times as necessary until the energy calmed down. I do not wish to alarm you. The strong spiritual text, from your own belief system will protect you, and being prepared, you will probably never have to use it!

In England every area has a trained priest who could assist in matters of exorcism. Contact your local bishop's office.

Chapter Fourteen

A sample Healing session

The doorbell rings a minute or two before two o'clock, the appointed time for my new client, Jane Brown, to arrive. I leave my dedicated Healing room, where things are ready to receive my new visitor. I have never seen her, know nothing about her and and have only spoken to her briefly on the telephone when she rang to make an appointment. I shall be seeing her alone, but, as she is a new client my husband is working in his office nearby. However the door is closed and the door of my Healing room is closed also, for my client must be assured of confidentiality.

I go to the front door looking neat and tidy but not over elaborately dressed or made up. I have my new client's name in mind and I welcome her with a smile, saying, "My name is Heather, and yours I believe is Jane. May I call you Jane?" I then take her coat and ask her how she is feeling today. I ask her to please follow me and I lead the way to my Healing room which is quite a large room with a sunny aspect. There is a large writing desk fairly centrally placed, which sounds quite formal, but it actually serves two purposes. As I work I often have the need for Reference books and also with me sitting on one side of the desk and my client on the other there is a neutral energy space between us, which is good. It is a shield for my aura. I don't know this person yet remember.

Now I take a new reference card and start taking personal details, Christian name by which the person likes to be known, and Surname, contact address and telephone number and then I ask her to tell me in just a few words why it is she feels she needs to see me. I purposely ask her to keep this brief. She explains that she has a frozen shoulder which she's had for eight months. She has had cortisone injections and is seeing a physiotherapist regularly, but is still on quite strong painkillers and nothing really seems to be helping.

I explain that the frozen shoulder is a secondary emanation of a primary cause and so I am going to be looking for the root causes of Jane's problem, and, in order to do that I shall need to take some energy readings from her. I take my pendulum in my right hand and I show her the Balance line. I show her that I merely have to think the word Balance and the pendulum starts to swing in a measured and regular way, away from me and towards me, and that it will continue to swing like this as long as it is required to do so. Having established Balance, I then say "But your All Over Energy is this." – Not knowing what is coming next, I watch to see what the pendulum gives me. The pendulum swiftly moves from Balance to the Lethargy Line. (This is a fictitious example but the pendulum has actually done this here and now. My guides are leading me through this as if I am dealing with a real person.) I explain that this reading means the person will be very low on energy and be very easily tired. As each energy reading comes up I record my findings in my duplicate book under the person's name and date. I explain that in the course of the session I shall be making brief notes about various things we speak of and the top copy of this they may take away with them, to remind them of the session. Sometimes we tape a session as well, if the client so wishes.

Jane confirms what I have said about her lack of energy and I then explain that this is the sum total of four different energies which I always identify for every client. These are Body energy, Everyday Mind energy, Spirit (in broad terms spiritual energy) and Deep Mind energy, which reveals to me what is going on in the unconscious mind. (It is the unconscious mind in this case, but is sometimes the subconscious mind.)

Her Body energy is – Just keep going it will be alright, settling on Fear/Pain. Jane explains she is basically afraid that she will lose her job. This is not because of her illness so much as because the firm she works for are themselves in difficulties. Fear/Pain in the Body energy is always indicative of pain in the actual physical body.

Jane's Everyday mind energy shows a forward position which is almost up to the Love/ Truth/ Healing/ Gift line, with a clockwise ellipse around it. This is slightly puzzling but I ask her if she is a creative person. She responds that she is. She loves to paint in her spare time, and although she is good she knows she somehow could be better.

How did I know what question to ask her about being a creative person? It was an insight in my head. I got painter or dancer in my head, and the pendulum quickly identified Painter, before she herself spoke. She is right, she could be better, but the pendulum pattern shows that in order to be better she will need to take a leap of faith and stop analysing her painting She needs to reach the Gift line, to make a full connection with the Divine energy, to take a leap of faith in her creativity The pendulum is on about 42 degrees already and there is the impetus to go forward, as shown in the ellipse. She has only a very short way to go and she's there on the wavelength, but in order to get there she has to be able to let go of control that last little bit. I explain all this and she seems very interested. She has already had moments of feeling a painting is "painting itself," that the result is better than she herself on her own is capable of. The jaded person who came to my door a short while ago is beginning to brighten up.

(Note that I don't actually have to measure angles. I have simply got to recognise them in non-specific general terms.)

Now we reach Spirit, or in its broadest sense spiritual, energy. The reading this time is, around about the Yes position (the underlying axis), again with an impetus to go forward, shown by the ellipse the pendulum describes. This person is interested in spiritual matters and would like to go farther, to find out more.

Deep mind. Here I see a certain boxed in pattern but it settles on the Balance line, in other words, and she confirms this when I challenge her with it, she is in a situation she knows she can't get out of, but she also knows that it is the will of God. She then goes on to explain that she has been with her husband many years and they work well together as a team, are extremely supportive of each other and have been very successful. It is their destiny to be together, but she has never been **deeply** in love with him.

As I am not told by my guides to go into any further energies for this person I turn to the Twelve Healers booklet and, holding the pendulum over the name of each remedy in turn, I see what comes up. I do not record any remedy which shows Balance. I am looking for negativity.

The first remedy I pick out is Aspen, with a boxed in negative pattern. I turn to the Bach Flower Therapy book by Mechthild Scheffer and the pendulum picks out: "The outward appearance of the aspen tree is a perfect symbol for the extreme sensitivity of the Aspen state. A breath of wind and the leaves are set rustling. You tremble like an aspen leaf. Aspen people react like a seismograph to the atmosphere in their visible and invisible environment."

Given this degree of sensitivity in the person and the situation both at work and at home, it is not surprising that Aspen might be required as a remedy, but we shall not know this for sure until all the remedies have been discovered.

The next remedy is Cerato and I am picking up a pattern that alternates between the Balance line and the Fear/Pain line. Cerato is connected to intuition and Right hand Feminine brain. It is a remedy for strengthening the intuition. The interpretation that comes into my mind for the pendulum swing is 'God fearing', and this the pendulum confirms as correct. This is an odd term in a way because I know it is more indicative of respect than fear on Jane's part. The Bach flower therapy book is once more referred to for insights and the pendulum picks out the final paragraph around Cerato, which states: "The seeds for subsequent Cerato states are often sown during schooldays, when the curriculum is too demanding, suppressing development of intuition in many children." My client explains that she was at a quite strictly run secondary school and she always had to work quite hard because the general standard of those pupils she was with was intellectually high. She is also, she admits, a person who tries to do her best.

The next remedy is Clematis on the Fear/Pain line. Clematis is a grounding remedy, a remedy for keeping us in the 'Here and now'. My client agrees that she is a bit of a worrier and wonders about what her future could be if the shoulder doesn't get better. I explain that being in the moment is very important because we **are** in the now anyway, but if at the same time we are living in the past or the future as well, and possibly worrying about it, then we are splitting our available energy, maybe in half! This is obviously one of the reasons for the Lethargy in her All over energy pattern. She explains that she has always been a worrier, in fact on her bedroom wall as a child was a little poker work plaque saying, 'Don't worry, it may never happen.'

The next remedy is Agrimony, on the No line, and one of the things around this remedy is that the person may drink too much alcohol in order to be able to cope with the difficulties of their life. This comes into my mind spontaneously for Jane, and so I gently challenge her with it. She agrees that she does rather over indulge with the wine, at times. She also realises that it is negatively affecting her, expressed by the No line, and agrees to moderate her habit.

The final remedy selected is Larch, registered as Anxious but OK. Larch is about the self – self image, self confidence, self worth and self esteem. In Jane's case I pick up on neither particularly, so once again I turn to the Bach flower Therapy book. The pendulum picks out the following – "Larch energy helps to dissolve the self-limiting, fixed concepts of the personality and permits the true potential to come to fruition. Somehow one is suddenly able to take a more 'relaxed' view of things and consider alternatives. The initiative can be taken, and the phrase 'I can't' disappears from the vocabulary. Continuing to assess things critically, but from what is basically a positive point of view, it is now possible to cope with almost every situation. A very human attitude develops, with one's own ego held in proper balance." This seems to us to relate largely to her home life, her work and her creativity, and we discuss the extent to which she may be able to 'free up' in her attitude to her painting. We laugh over our use of the words 'free up', especially when applied to her frozen shoulder!

Now we have five remedies, selected from thirty eight and the client understands why they are all there and how they refer to her at this time in her life. However, as a final check, I start with the All over Lethargy line energy on the pendulum, and show Jane how, as I add the name of each remedy in turn the pendulum changes position, moving closer and closer to the Healing Line until with the final addition of Larch, the Healing Line is reached. This proves to me that the correct remedies have been chosen at this time to bring about healing for Jane *and* her shoulder.

I would then proceed to ask Jane if she would like some healing, and this I am going to give you as a simple example, as you yourself might be able to do, following the information in this book at an elementary level.

You have only the first and second choice sets of crystals and they are carefully laid out on the desk in the right order.

Start with the shoulder first. The problem is in the left shoulder by the way. The throat chakra is identified by the pendulum and the choice of crystals is either blue lace agate or aquamarine. The pendulum picks aquamarine. You may be able to get the pendulum to show you where to put the crystal by moving your index finger of the left hand over the shoulder and watching for the Healing line on the pendulum. If you don't feel confident enough for this, just ask your client where the pain is. The client at this point should still be sitting comfortably in her chair. This makes it easy for you to reach her shoulder. Having cleared with your client that she is alright with being touched, place the crystal on a point where she experiences pain, or on the point the pendulum indicates to you. The pendulum is likely to start swinging on the Fear/Pain line, identifying the pain. Then ask it to show you the Healing line when the crystal has been correctly placed, and to give you the Balance Line when the healing is finished. It is quite alright to ask these things in your head rather than audibly. Alternatively you could pull your left hand away from the body until you get the healing line and then proceed with the healing with your hand held at that position.

With your client still sitting in her chair, ask her to hold both hands out in front of her on her lap, palms upturned in an expression of asking and openness. This time you are going to be working *above* her head, the purpose of which is to channel the Divine Healing Energy right down through your client's whole body, bringing the body energies together wholistically. The pendulum may well start from the All over energy pattern of Lethargy that your client came to you with, but should quite quickly move around to the Healing Line without the use of a crystal. If it does not, hold your crown chakra crystal in your left hand while you work. It continues to swing on that line while the healing energy is being delivered and you are "waiting patiently on that person." Sometimes the phrase, "Make me a channel of Thy peace." comes into my head. When the healing energy has been delivered the pendulum returns to Balance to show that clearly, and you make your affirmation to the Divine Source, however you wish to express it. (In the name of God, Allah, Gaia, Cosmic Mind, Whatever name you feel comfortable with, in order to name the Higher Power for you. Amen.)

This, as I have explained, is a very simple form of healing, much simpler than my usual way of working, but it can still be manageable and beneficial, to your client. Sometimes when you use crystals for healing there will be a message in one of them, so get used to that from the beginning. In this case we have only used the aquamarine, but never the less I am told there is a message in it for Jane. This message will be from her guide or guardian angel. To obtain it for her I turn to the wonderful book on crystals, to me there is no other like it, " Love is in the Earth, a kaleidoscope of crystals." Hold the pendulum over the text and, in my terms, trawl down the page. At a certain point the pendulum goes over on to the Healing/Truth Line.

The message for Jane is as follows – "It provides for access to stored information concerning the perfection of the body and enhances ones insight into the art and practice of actualising the perfection; it provides for inspiration and for an inculcation of the truths of the universe and the universal perfection."

My advice to Jane would be, if possible, to go out and buy herself an aquamarine, either to wear or to carry around with her in a little velvet bag.

Chapter Fifteen

Frequently asked Questions

Q. Could I use the pendulum for lottery numbers?

A. The lottery and similar situations where people, through no effort or skill of their own, find themselves suddenly in possession of a great deal of money or power, can be a very difficult and, in spiritual growth terms at least, a dangerous place to be. The influences which truly guide the pendulum in order to communicate to us in a loving creative way, wanting only what is best for us, are not going to get involved in such a venture, and therefore if the pendulum moves at all, I personally would be very reluctant indeed to take any notice.

––––––––

Q. Do you think that animals go to Heaven?

A. There is a continuation and regeneration of all life. Nothing is lost to the system. What goes around comes around, and what we sow, that shall we reap. I think where we find ourselves after we leave this life is all a matter of the discipline we have applied to ourselves to overcome the base in us, the effort we have made to always do our best, and good old "stickability". Having said that, I know that the Light Beings on the other side of Life have a good sense of humour and want us to have fun. All sentient beings have a contract and a responsibility directly to the Higher Power, that we do not abuse, but rather use that which we are given. There are many stories of animals doing heroic incredible feats, using amazing powers of love and insight, wonderfully aiding their human counterparts. This surely will not be either overlooked or discarded. I was once told by a medium I visited that my daughter had received a cat I had sent her. She first asked me if I had a daughter in Spirit, which I confirmed. Then she went on to describe our daughter and continued with, "She's holding up a cat and saying, "I've got the cat Mum." Only I knew this was true. I live many miles away in Cornwall and about a fortnight before, a lady who had been

159

to me several times for healing rang me and spoke about her dearly beloved elderly cat. She asked me if I could find out through the pendulum whether this little animal wished to move on to the next dimension. I was able to confirm for her through the pendulum that this was in fact so, to which she replied that I had given her the courage to do that which she felt herself to be right and so the vet was called to her home. And now here was the medium telling me that my daughter had the cat in her care and safekeeping. The medium went on to describe the cat, which I had never seen. However, on my return home I rang the owner and explained what had happened. She was of course delighted and confirmed from the description I gave that this was indeed the cat! I had received evidence of continuation of life of an animal for myself.

I have also had experience of people in Regression going forward from a life as a human to one of an animal, and vice versa, that is to say from the life of an animal to one of a human being. This is not necessarily a matter of promotion or demotion, but rather a desire of the soul to experience all things. We may even sometime in the future wish to experience being a small insect, and if we truly believed this were possible it would surely give us a reverence for all life forms.

Q. When you are healing what are you thinking about?

A. First of all I prefer to say, "When I am being used as a channel for healing energy," but to answer the question, my focus is on being that channel and so, "Make me a channel of Thy Peace" might come spontaneously into my head. Or I might be working with a particular illness, for example a cancer of a particular type, and so I may be guided to appeal for a guide, who maybe, while still in incarnation, was an expert in this field. I believe that after we pass over we can still be very aware of what is going on in this dimension and have both an ability and a desire to help others still in incarnation. Also I believe that what endures is our personality, which defines us, and what we have learnt.

I feel that my usage of crystals is accurate. My confirmation for that is that when one is identified by the guide as having a message in it, the message is *so accurate and relevant to what has taken place in the session.*

My job really is to have a state of mind which is like a blank screen, so that the guides can pass me any information they choose, for me to pick up on, like, "Use the piece of amber here." or "Place this particular piece of lapis lazuli there." The information is always very specific, and is cross checked by getting the Truth line on the pendulum. All this happens quickly, without hesitation, so that there is no break in the flow of the work.

Q. If I'm having difficulty, at any time, tuning in to a person or a situation, is there any extra advice or help you could give me?

A. This reminds me of my early days of dowsing, when I used to find the same problem. The difficulty is in establishing whether or not the task is possible for you. What I did was to ask for a circle if it was possible for me to work with the situation. For example people would phone me and ask if I could help them with this problem or that, and of course I didn't know the answer, but the guides did, so I used to ask them to give me a circle there and then if I *could* help. For a while I also used this means of alignment of our two energies before I started work with anyone. Later on I was able to work with whatever problem came along.

––––––––––

Q. How do crystals work?

A. When placed on or around the body with the intention of being used for healing, crystals act as a rite of passage to certain incoming energies. I often say that they are like keyholes which will only allow a specific key to enter and unlock the situation. While healing the body, and I should more correctly say "bodies" here, I am looking, by means of the pendulum and the index finger of my left hand used as a pointer, for specific places where the flow of Chi energy around the body is impaired. When I find a point such as this, it may be possible simply to apply the appropriate crystal, (its name will be dropped into my mind, and I crosscheck for Truth by means of the pendulum,) whereupon the energy switches immediately around to the Healing line. I then cover the crystal with my left hand until the Healing energy at that physical level has been delivered. However, further correction of energy, at more subtle levels of healing further from the physical body, may be required. The pendulum passes me this information by means of either the Yes line with positive Working/Thinking energy around it, or merely a clockwise circle (Working/Thinking.) In this context these patterns constitute a 'Keep going' message.

––––––––––

Q. What do you mean by further correction at more subtle levels, and how can you effect this correction?

A. By this I mean correction within the different bodies in the aura, or energy field around the physical body. I don't actually concern myself greatly with the names of these bodies, but they are Physical, Etheric, Emotional, Mental, Astral, Etheric template (physical aspect), Celestial (emotional aspect), Ketheric (mental aspect). Each of these in turn is a little further out from the physical body. They are linked to the chakras, in order, as follows – Root/red, Sacral/orange, Solar

161

plexus/yellow, Heart/ green or pink, Throat/ blue, Third Eye/ indigo, Crown/violet. I merely know that I have to clear the energy to the very extreme of the auric space and try to ensure that no negative energy still lurks there. Sometimes to remove the last little bit can be tricky. Some negative energies do not give in easily, because they feed on existing the situation and do not want to be cast out for transformation. An excellent book for information on the energy bodies is "Hands of Light", a guide to Healing through the Human energy field, by Barbara Ann Brennan.

How I effect this clearing out from the physical body form is by still using the original crystal placed on the physical body at that point. If the original site was difficult in that I have had to hold the crystal in place there, then I continue to hold the crystal, pulling it directly out from the body surface until I reach a point where the pendulum is once again giving me the healing line. We work here once more until the healing energy has been delivered and then I watch for further information from the pendulum of a clockwise circle, if I have to work still further out in the aura. The sign that the work is finished is the Balance Line, which is cross checked by me, using the Truth Line. When working on a client by means of Hands On healing, I start working at the soles of the feet and continue right up over the body to a point somewhere above the head. This final position varies with each person, as some are able to stand more subtle but powerful energies than others, and this can vary not only from person to person, but from day to day. (Refer to chapter eight.)

A very special friend and I have just been discussing plum bobs and she said, and I quote, " Are we not building the Soul of the Universe, while we build our own souls?" It is certainly a point to ponder. As for bodies, on a microcosmic level all the cells in the body are continually renewing themselves and on a macroscopic level The heavenly bodies are continually dying and being born also. Therefore why do we find it so difficult to accept the idea of reincarnation? I have just been told that body cells can be renewed according to the Matrix. (Yes, capital M and all!) This has come as a, "voice in my head". Going to the dictionary, (Chambers 20th Century Dictionary), I have looked up the word Matrix. It says, "The womb, the cavity in which anything is formed,........A rectangular array of quantities or symbols (math)....matrix, a breeding animal, later, the womb, mater, '(Latin) mother.' From this, through the pendulum, I get that cells can be renewed according to the Female aspect of the Creative Divine. (The pendulum swings on the Truth Line at this point.) This renewal of cells is fundamental in Healing and if this is so, the condition and well-being of a cell can be changed by the Matrix, in other words by Feminine aspect of the Divine Will, either way, or as we might say, either positively or negatively. Whichever way the change occurs, it will always, I believe, be in order to serve the Best and Highest Good. The receipt of information in this way may seem extraordinary to you at this moment in time, but it is what the whole of my work is based upon.

Q. When you use the term, "Pull out" in conjunction with negative energies, "Pull out, or cast out where?

A. This is a very important point. The negative energy drawn out from the client's bodies must ALWAYS handed over to the Transforming Angel there and then, or you could name this powerful force for transformation, from negative to positive, in a different way if the term angel makes you feel uncomfortable. My shamanic friend would probably say it was being taken off to the volcano for purification! But that's fine by me. She's only using different words to describe the same energy I believe. What you definitely do NOT do is cast negative energy out into the ether with nowhere to go and no direction. All energy has the potential for transformation and LOVE, even for the so-called negative Energy, is always the answer.

Q. Do you ever work without using a crystal aid?

A. Yes I still do sometimes. There were years of Healing work that went on before I started to use crystals, but once I started I never looked back because they switch the energy much faster and more efficiently. However, sometimes during a healing I will only use my hands.

Say I have discovered some negative energy, (registering on the pendulum, which is always held in my right hand) but the instruction is not to use a crystal, instead it is to "pull out", and I will hear this in my head, always then confirmed by the Truth line. Here I get to go straight down to the surface of the body and pull out the offending negativity, to a distance of maybe fifteen to twenty inches from the body, using a closed hand shape, as if I was pulling on a piece of string. This action may need to be repeated several times while monitoring the situation with the pendulum, held in the other hand. On each pull the pendulum goes further around from a negative position, (which could have been Negative, Fear/Pain, or even Lethargy to start with) to a more positive position, ending up, if possible on the Healing line, or even better, the full Working /Thinking pattern. Basically you have to work with the negativity you find, and make it as positive as you can.

Sometimes if I am working up the body, say maybe the legs, I may find a spot that is just a little negative, and I know that I can rectify the situation by just one or two simple pullouts without the aid of a crystal - quicker and simpler.

Q. Do you ever use both hands to heal?

A. Yes. There are times when this is my instruction. Using both hands sends the energy specifically THROUGH the body. There are actually many chakras in the body and these are not sitting on the surface. They have fronts and backs. Say I was working on a damaged knee joint. I might be told to use a certain crystal in order to get the energy "running", that's to say working on the Healing line. To do this, the crystal is gently rubbed to nudge it awake, and then applied to a specific point on the knee joint. Once the crystal has established the Healing Line energy, I may hear a message, for example "Use both hands." So I drop the pendulum and place one hand on one side of the knee joint and one hand on the other, while telling the person that my intention is to send the healing energy through the joint. Being instructed as closely as this, you can be sure that something specific and beneficial will be happening.

In connection with this point, there are times, when the client is lying on their back that I may get a sense of the need for the energy to be passed specifically through the body. They may be known to have a back problem for example. Healing is about intention and so I can ask for the healing to be passed through the body when the specific hand positions would not be possible. Of course if a person was known to have a back problem you might well choose to work with a specific site before they lay down for the all over body balancing, as well.

Q. Do some people come to you simply wanting you to heal, for example, their sore leg and not investigate their emotional lives? If so what would you do?

A. I would comply with their request. I am here to help people at the level at which they feel ready. The fact that they are able to ask for help at all is a step along the way. In actual fact though this situation almost never happens. Most people are fascinated with the possibility of what happens here and really enjoy their session. It's amazing really, the difference in attitude between coming here for help and most people's attitude to going to a doctor's surgery, for example.

However what I would say is that healing, real lasting healing, is about enlightenment and emotional adjustment. The physical aspect in the body is merely a by-product of that. Christ, when administering healing in the Bible says, "Go thy way and sin no more." He gets picked up by the Pharisees, or Church leaders saying, "What right has this man to forgive sins?" Now, I'm not in the business of forgiving sins, but I am in the business of being shown by my guides where the person's mistakes (missing of the marks, sins) are, and in being competent at passing that information on to them for their consideration.

You may think, "What has a bad leg to do with all this?" But what if one of the remedies was Rock Water, in the group, "Over-care for the welfare of others," (working too hard) and what if the piece picked out in the Mechthild Scheffer book was, "Trying to meet exaggerated self imposed standards........ conceitedness, a sublime form of spiritual pride, a self-righteousness." (Feeling that they are the only person who can correctly help others.) Is it any wonder this person has a bad leg! Or at least that their way of thinking comes out somewhere! My job would then be to kindly and without any sense of judgement, point out what I had been shown. This would enlighten the person and so, not only would the pain in the leg be no longer necessary to point out the error, but hopefully the error itself would be corrected.

Q. Healing is sometimes called Faith Healing. Do I need to have faith in order to be healed?

A. No. I am the one who needs the unshakeable faith in the source of the healing processes and in the healing processes themselves. All I require from my client is that they be open minded, open to the possibility of change.

Q. Is it ever too late for people to be helped?

A. No. Change can occur right up to the time we draw our last breath........ and beyond!

Q. How do you deal with the high levels of emotions you must sometimes get from your clients?

A. By staying very calm in all circumstances. These people trust me and need me to be there, solid as a rock. That does not mean that there will not be times when the emotions flow out of them with abandon, like a river. Sometimes I say a few words to them and the floodgates are opened. I do not then immediately rush in with the paper hankies, saying, "There, there", because it is important that people are allowed to feel their feelings. It may be the first opportunity they have had to do so. However, do not let it go on for too long. Keep the tissues and the Rescue Remedy handy. These simple measures often allow the session to continue normally after only a few minutes.

Q. What helps you stay sufficiently balanced yourself, so that you can so frequently be there for others?

A. Having a good and supportive family is very important to me. Also the stillness and calm centredness, which is so much a part of the Quaker Faith, is important, including the support my meeting gives me in the work that I do. As a Quaker I have become accustomed to working from a still centre within me. I have learned besides to "clear as I go". This means that if I have a worry or a problem of my own I address it and deal with it.

Q. How do you decide how often a person needs to see you?

A. The answer to this is twofold. Let's deal with the space between appointments first. For many years I was working away on my own and there was only so much time I could give in the three days a week I could spare. Four two hour sessions was all I could manage a day – there was a limit as to what I could offer in terms of time. Most people therefore see me once a month or so. There is no point is seeing the person too often in my experience, because the remedies dispensed bring up a lot of psychological material for the client and that takes time to process. It is not advisable to change the prescription too frequently otherwise this vital process will not be completed. On a second visit the energy situations and the remedies needed to counteract them will be entirely different. That is how it should be.

Because of this, once a month is normal for me. However there are occasions where the client is in a desperate situation to start with and these people may need seeing once a week or even more often in the beginning, because the situation is changing so rapidly.

Secondly, in order to help us decide how many sessions people need with me, I group three sessions together as a treatment. When a client first comes neither of us knows how long the Healing support will need to go on, but it is important that it doesn't go on longer than necessary. The aim is for my client to be able to 'stand on their own feet' and not become reliant on me. That is not good for them and it's not good for me because it doesn't free me up to move on and help others. On the other hand I don't want to take away the support too early, so that the problem comes back. If I feel my client is becoming to dependent, I set a limit, so that they know they are on their last treatment before we take a break. I assure them that I will still be there if they need me, and they can always come back should they need to do so, but we both need to see how they manage on their own for a while.

———

Q. Is there any way we can go through life without pain?

A. "There is only one road to true human greatness : the road through suffering." – Albert Einstein 1947, commenting on the plight of the African Americans.

I believe, along with the Buddhists, that our pain is caused by our attachment. Therefore the way of dispensing with pain is to refuse to be too attached to anything (or anybody). There is an anomaly here however because we know we are all part of each other, part of the One. However I have many times said that I feel the big lesson of life is to learn to stand alone, complete, without need, but then again, as the great poet John Donne said, "No man is an island" And so we can keep flipping this situation over and over..........

The fact of the matter is that we do all experience pain from time to time and pain is a great indicator. Use it like a red light and when it comes stop and think. Think, "what is the message of this pain? What is the pain trying to make me aware of? Where is the error?" Many people push on through pain and cause untold damage by so doing.

———

Q. Could you give me an example of dealing with pain in an emergency?

A. A non-invasive way of handling one's own pain or helping another person in pain in an emergency is illustrated by the following example.

Once I found myself sitting next to a young woman on an aeroplane, who started to have severe pains in her head. She had told me earlier that she was worried about the flight because she had had about three weeks of really bad sinusitis, to which I had replied lightly "Oh, don't worry, I'm a healer." She was an art lecturer at university and I was just returning from a visit to Germany, where an exhibition of art had been shown, my work and that of my fellow travellers, and so we had a very interesting conversation until pain did in fact start bothering her and she went very quiet. At this point I got the pendulum swinging on the Healing Line and then asked her to catch hold of my left hand. The moment she did that the pain in her head eased right back and soon disappeared altogether, and we were able to resume our conversation, but we continued to sit in contact like that for well over an hour, and only as the plane touched down on the tarmac did the pendulum stop swinging of its own accord. She happened to be a lecturer at university, and, as she was totally amazed at what had happened, she said she was going to recount the incident to her students the next day to see how they would react. Distant healing is also possible in this way when actual physical contact is not possible. For example, you can send another person love in the form of a prayer, or even send it over the telephone by the pendulum swinging on the Healing Line, but don't forget to make the affirmation afterwards!

———

Q. How do you clear both yourself and your clinic of any emotional trauma that may hang around?

A. First of all, I do this by keeping the space as clean, tidy and fresh as I can. These aspects are indicators of the practitioner's state of mind and general efficiency and does not encourage dark forces to linger. Other than that, I would prefer to use sound. There are lots of ways one could use but the way that works best is the ritual with which you, the practitioner feels most comfortable. If something really difficult had occurred in my clinic I would open the window and door as soon as possible afterwards. I would then repeat out loud the Lord's Prayer, while holding the pendulum until I got the Balance Line on the pendulum. If this wasn't sufficient I would then move on to repeating out loud the Twenty- third Psalm, and if even that didn't sufficiently work I would use my xylophone note of E1 by striking it in all four corners of the room in the name of the **Divine Creator**, that being a **very** powerful name indeed in the world of Spirit, and most entities will bow to it.

As for myself, I can wrap myself in a golden orb, with a wonderfully glowing pink light around it, but trust is a very important word and I trust my guides with my life.

––––––––––

Q. Thinking of the word Life, you say that there is nobody who cannot be helped, if they are open to help, at any time, right up to the very end of their life. People are often afraid of the possibility of intolerable pain, towards the end. Could you say something about a client's management of pain?

A. Pain can be managed clinically these days, often by the patient themselves, using little machines that deliver substances such as morphine on demand. The fact that the patient is in control quite often means that less of the pain-dulling substance is needed because the element of fear, of pain being left unattended, is removed. However, we are talking esoterically here and so drugs may not be being used. One of the things I have found helpful is obviously anything which helps to remove any element of fear from the situation, (Fear and Pain come in on the same wavelength remember.) Anything at all which is on the patient's mind, for example, unresolved problems with relationships, needs, if possible, to be healed. Pain can also be integrated into the body instead of being pushed away. This can be done by means of colour. Think of the colours of the rainbow, starting with red. Progress though the colours of orange, yellow, green, pink, turquoise, blue, indigo, violet, magenta, white, silver and gold. Try each colour out carefully before moving to the next one. Focus it in the area where you have the pain, and you will often find that one of the colours makes the energy you refer to as pain feel very different in that area, and subsequently the pain disappears or very much diminishes.

You may wonder how relationships can be healed if the person with whom the difficulty exists cannot be reached, maybe is not even any longer alive themselves. A solution here is to write to the person, expressing, as exactly as you can, how you have been feeling. If you now think those feelings are unworthy of you, then you can ask for the person's forgiveness. If, on the other hand you think they have treated you wrongly in the past you may be able to say that you now better understand the difficulties and pressures they were under at the time and find it in your heart, at least in part, to forgive them. These writings should then be buried, burnt, or otherwise destroyed, to represent the fact that for you, there is an end of the matter.

This communication could be even more important for the person in Spirit than it is for the person here. Sometimes the person in Spirit needs a forgiveness and a blessing from our world, around their wrong doings, before they are able to move on.

Ideally the atmosphere at the end should be one of peace, beauty and loving kindness, trying to maintain a high level of purity of thought and positivity of mind, surrounding a person who is dying. Flowers, gentle music that the person has been known to love, may be quietly played. Integration with one's surroundings is the aim, so do not have anything, or anybody present that the dying person would wish to push away. Finally, as a healer, do not see death as failure. Death is the doorway to a new and wonderful life, a doorway to a place where we are truly at home.

Q. How can I best go about learning the language of movement contained in this book?

A. The language of movement contained in this book is a gift. It is a gift in physical form which has come, I believe, from an intelligent source. I have received it and used it over many years and now I pass it on to you. It may or may not be complete, but it is as complete as I can make it at this moment in time. It should be treated in the same way as any other gift, that is to say, first and foremost it should be used with honour and impeccability. The rules and skill need to be learned with patience, and having been learned, are best forgotten. By that I mean that you get to know the language so well that you do not have to remember it and think about it because it is automatic. It is when your skill reaches this point that the gift can take off once more and become individual to you, offering you even more insights than before. As I have said many times in sessions with clients, gift is about **not doing it thinking**, for thinking is working with logical mind, but gift is connected to intuitive right hand brain, where fresh information can be passed to you from a source which lies beyond the small self.

Q. Have you personally had any strange experiences?

A. I have had very many. They occur on an almost daily basis. I seem to live in the space between the worlds and another whole book could be written on the subject, so maybe it will be!

A second book on Regression/Progression techniques using extended pendulum language, and illustrated with numerous fascinating transcriptions of sessions with clients is now in preparation. This book will hopefully be released in 2006. For details, please check the website: www.keystowisdom.co.uk

★★★★★★★

I conclude my dissertation with the following words habitual with oriental authors when explaining a doctrine:
"If my readers find unintelligibility and mistakes in my account, the fault is mine who have not been able to express, as they ought to have been, the Teachings which were communicated to me."

★★★★★★★

Bibliography

THE TWELVE HEALERS and Other Remedies.   Edward Bach
Pub C.W. Daniel Company Ltd.
I Church Path, Saffron Walden, Essex, England.

BACH FLOWER THERAPY The Complete Approach
Mechthild Scheffer
Pub Thorsons *an imprint* of Harper Collins *Publishers*
ISBN 0-7225-1121-3

NEW BACH FLOWER BODY MAPS
DIETMAR KRAMER and Helmut Wild
Pub HEALING ARTS PRESS   ROCHESTER, VERMONT
ISBN 0-89281-531-0

AMBIKA'S GUIDE TO HEALING AND WHOLENESS
The Energetic Path to Chakras and Colour
Pub PIATKUS
ISBN 0-7499-1290-1

CHAKRA HEALING   LIZ SIMPSON
Pub GAIA
ISBN 1-856750-83-3

THE ELEMENTS OF THE CHAKRAS   Naomi Ozaniec
Pub ELEMENT
ISBN 1-85230-174-0

HEALING WITH COLOUR   Theo Gimbal
Pub GAIA
ISBN 1-85675-063-9

LOVE IS IN THE EARTH   A KALEIDOSCOPE OF CRYSTALS
UPDATED
EARTH LOVE PUBLISHING HOUSE
3440 Youngfield Street, Suite 353
Wheat Ridge, CO. 80033
ISBN 0-9628190-3-4

WHO IS YOUR GUARDIAN ANGEL? VERONIQUE JARRY
WARNER BOOKS   ISBN 0-446-67385-4

ANGEL SIGNS   A Celestial Guide To The Powers Of Your
Own Guardian Angel
Albert Haldane and Simha Seraya with Barbara Lagowski
Harper San Francisco
ISBN 0-06-251706-6

A Dictionary of Angels   Gustav Davidson
Pub Free Press
ISBN 0-02-907052-X   An excellent reference book

The Medical Discoveries of Edward Bach Physician   Nora Weeks
CW Daniel Company Ltd
ISBN 85027- 001- 2

HANDS OF LIGHT - A guide to healing through the human energy field
B A Brennan
Bantam New Age Books ISBN 0-553-34539-1

The Secret Oral Teachings in Tibetan Buddhist Sects
Alexandra David-Neel and Lama Yongden.
Published by City Lights Books, San Francisco.   ISBN 0-87286-012-4